Up The Wooden Hill

A Tale of Two Families

CHAPTER 1

Years of undisturbed dust enshrouded the stacks of stored treasures long forgotten in the attic of the big old house on the avenue of a London suburb. The red, white and blue stripes, usually bright and vivid, of a tiny patriotic Union Jack flag, flung forlornly to the floorboards, were scarcely distinguishable beneath the pall of gray. The stark swastika insignia on the cover of a booklet close by no longer appeared bold and black. Only the piles of luggage, peppered with powdery dust particles, appeared to have had any recent use.

A creaking footstep on the ladder below, a squeak of hinges rusty from rest, and the muffled voice of an intruder suddenly disturbed the quiet peace of the gloomy place. As the heavy trap door opened, a rustling sigh of fresh air wafted up through the yawning hole. Groping fingers found and flicked on a light switch at the head of the ladder, illuminating the gloomy attic. Obscure shapes sprang startlingly to life.

"Hooray," Jill cheered, spotting the suitcases as her head emerged above the attic floor. "Looks like Mother was right and I'm in luck." Climbing carefully from the top of the ladder, she stepped across the cavernous opening and stood upright to survey the scene. Although pleased to have found the suitcases, she looked in dismay at the piles of photo albums, cardboard cartons, shoe boxes and tatty, dog-eared manila envelopes, all stuffed to overflowing, and wondered where to start looking for her family mementos. Nondescript items and a few photographs lay around loosely among the dust balls. Wrinkling her nose to ward off a tickling sneeze, Jill was surprised that the attic was not piled high to the rafters. Her mother, an avid saver and salvager since the days of wartime austerity, never ever threw anything away.

As Jill stepped gingerly toward the assortment of suitcases, her toe pushed against the Nazi booklet on the floor. It slithered and flipped over to land up alongside the faded flag which waved weakly at the onslaught. She paused, stared down, then stooped to scoop them up. Wondering what she'd found, she blew off the dust and smiled as she recognized the mementoes. "What a find," she murmured, pocketing them in her cardigan to take downstairs with the suitcases and any other interesting souvenirs she might discover among the dusty collection lying silently around her.

"Everything must still be up here since I first left home nearly thirty years ago," she thought, remembering that her parents had moved to this house from the one across the road right after her wedding.

None of the family, her father and three brothers had wanted to move from their charming cottage-style home to the larger mansion type, but Mother was adamant about moving from the 'wrong side of the road' to the 'sunny side of the street' so important to the sun-starved English. Besides, it would be easier to visit her three sisters and families who already lived across the heavily trafficked road. So after ten years of brightening up the home on the 'wrong side' with a bright red front door and widening windows to catch the elusive sun, Mother finally persuaded her husband to leave his flowery back garden paradise to start anew.

Jill remembered the strangeness of visiting from her new home in Germany to turn into the driveway across from her old home. Little did she know that both she and Horst would soon embrace the new house as home when they returned for the birth of their first son and her parent's first grandchild. "Hmm," she thought, looking around the jumble of possessions. "I bet Mother even kept our gasmasks from the war. Now that's ancient history if anything is!" Jill's memories unfolded...

She bent down to push everything together like a pack of playing cards, a difficult feat because of their varying sizes. Her eye caught the gray shadows, stark blacks and contrasting whites of scattered photos. "How dusty everything is," she said with a loud sneeze which echoed throughout the empty attic and scattered a few photos onto the floor. She picked up one that showed a small group of smiling faces. Recognizing it as one of the many photos taken in Germany, her new homeland after her marriage, this showed the celebration of her brawny, blue-collared brother-in-law's birthday.

Beginning at three in the afternoon with coffee, cake, congratulatory speeches, joke-telling and opening of presents, the party went on until ten at night. That was the first time Jill had seen her young husband, the greatly loved son and older brother, with his entire family as he played the role of life and soul of the party, family jester and nonstop entertainer. It became a common sight for his married sister to slip off the sofa collapsing in uncontrollable shrieks of laughter at her brother's hilarious jokes and clowning.

Goblets of white wine, steins of beer and a smorgasbord of sausage, cheese and pickled fish—a veritable feast for anyone who favours delicatessens—followed the tea-time celebration. More raucous humour and loud laughter arose after each joke, all elaborately translated by her husband for her benefit. The family, immediately silent and wide-eyed in expectation of her delirious reaction, hung onto every syllable as Jill clung to every word of a humour totally different from her own dry British wit. Besides that, the punch line always got lost in the translation.

So after seven long, loud hours with her head spinning and a smile frozen to her lips, angry resentment at her inability to understand a single word, replaced polite patience. To everyone's astonishment she rushed from the room into the cool night air followed by her young husband who unaware of her strain and tension, quickly comforted her "They meant kindly, I know," remembered Jill, forgiving the ordeal of those trying times.

"How flattered I'd felt," thought Jill, remembering her own birthday when her new German family had sung the old familiar 'Happy Birthday' song in their oddly accented words 'Har-pee Burst-day Too Yoo'. And how disillusioned she'd felt on joining in the same refrain for her brother-in-law, only to realize that they hadn't sung it especially in English for her. They considered it their own song, anyway! How often had she since wondered why a melodious nation like Germany with its expansive repertoire of songs for every occasion and mood, had no birthday song of its own!

The German language, especially when heard as an unintelligible loud and strident garble, at first sounded to her as if everyone was angry and arguing. "How amazed I was to peep around the kitchen door to see smiling faces seated around the wooden table, drinking coffee or wine and happily chatting," she mused

"Well, it must have been as difficult for them as it was for me being thrust into their midst—the oldest son's new foreign bride with not a word of German and they with little to no English." Laughing to herself Jill realized what a long way she had come since those days. "I must show this to Horst," she said, pocketing the photo.

Next to the suitcases she needed was a stack of loose-leaf sheets of paper covered in typing, which looked strangely familiar. Jill stopped in her tracks.

"Oh, no, not that!" she cried, and turned away. "I'm not going to get involved with that masterpiece again."

"Hoisted by his own petard," she chuckled. Her husband had at first encouraged her in her new hobby of writing a memoir until it took all her time and energy, the housekeeping went undone and she was never available for a game of tennis or an evening of dancing. His tolerance soon turned to impatience. She laughed as she recalled her artful answer of "Polishing, dear," when he asked what she was doing shut away in the bedroom. It hadn't taken him long to realize that it was her writing getting the polishing, not the furniture!

Jill crouched down, quickly picking up and perfunctorily examining what was hers and discarding anything else. She found the family tree, miscellaneous magazines and memorabilia as well as her mother's photo album upon which her book was based. Time passed quickly as she rummaged, sorted and stacked, and was soon ready to return with her finds to life below the attic.

Her memoir lay on top of one of the piles to be left behind. Unable to resist any longer, she picked it up and glanced through the family annals. Although fresh and familiar, she felt something was lacking. She continued reading. A few chapters along Jill paused, put down the book, beamed and said, "That's it. That's what it needs!"

She had an idea. Coupled with her memories of Germany and how she had started out in that country after meeting and marrying Horst, she realized that if he would tell his parallel life story, that would add the extra oomph to the book. He could start with his birth in Berlin, on through the war years in Ludwigshafen on the Rhine and up until they both met in London.

Delighted with the idea, Jill started to pack up, eager to put her plan into action. "I'll take my memoir down with the rest of the stuff, and at the right moment bring it out and casually quote from my writings," she thought as she worked. "I know Horst can come up with a parallel story—an even better one, I bet! I've just got to catch him at the right moment and get him to talk. I'll seduce him into talking and reminiscing about his childhood in Berlin—and take it from there!"

CHAPTER 2

Balanced precariously on the middle rungs of the ladder, her head still in the confines of the dark hole above, Jill paused to adjust the piled-high stack of dusty treasures wedged tightly under her chin. One hand supported from underneath, while the other clutched the suitcases, one inside the other.

Impatient to get down, sort through her discoveries and to put her plan into action, Jill tried to make the difficult descent from the attic in one go. Walking backwards down the rickety ladder without a handrail was a balancing feat. She swayed under the load. The carefully retrieved spoils shifted slightly, then all of a sudden slipped, scattering out of her clutching grasp to land with a soft thud on the carpeted landing below. All now lay in a jumble far worse than the one in which they had long lain undisturbed.

On reaching the bottom of the ladder, Jill put down the suitcases and turned with a sigh to face the disorderly scene of dog-eared photo albums, a mysterious dusty shoe box and several large tattered manila envelopes, all stuffed with mementoes. The leaves of her book were awry but still intact.

The contents of the box, spilled out higgledy-piggledy at her feet, caught her attention. She picked up a little newspaper clipping, a news article portraying a young couple standing side by side and gazing at each other. The caption in capital letters read—LONDON ROMANCE. Below the picture ran a short article.

"Language student Horst Schaefer, 25, came to Britain from Germany seven weeks ago to study English for three months. He visited Speaker's Corner, Hyde Park, on his second day here and met 24 year old Miss Jill Martin, who had come home to London on holiday after five years in the United States. Now they are to marry at St. Dunstan's Church, Ealing, on Sunday."

Jill smiled fondly at the young engaged couple, both tall and slim. "How terribly thin poor old Horst was," she murmured. "I'd no idea that he was recovering from an ulcer when I met him. I thought he was a health fanatic, watching his weight with special foods. But, of course, I can see how the strain of our wedding—with the abundance of hard liquor—to a sensitive young man from the wine-growing area of Germany, would cause a relapse. What a honeymoon!

A deep voice from below interrupted her thoughts. "What was all that noise about?" A handsome head popped up from the staircase below, an older and rounder version of the young man in the newspaper. Soft-faced, smiling and in his late forties, with a neat graying goatee, his close-cropped hair was soft and silvery like his mother's, all atop his father's long legs. Jill would tease her husband by calling him 'Oma (Granny in German) – 'Oma on Stilts'.

"What on earth have you got there, Jill?" he asked, looming ever taller as he reached the landing and surveyed the fallen debris on the floor. "I thought you went up for a suitcase!"

"Yes, I did," she retorted, pointing to the suitcases. "I found them and brought down these two—and more besides," she added, thinking of the time she had spent gleaning over her discoveries. "Mother suggested I do some sorting out up there," she explained. She fished out the German birthday photo and handed it to him, thinking it might get him interested. "Remember, twenty-three—or four—years ago?"

Horst took the photo. A smile spread over his face as he recognized the scene. "How young we all look, and adding gallantly, "You especially, liebling, Haven't changed a bit. Still as slim as ever."

"You know, Horst, I really considered myself fashionably thin and willowy when I first went over to Germany. But remember what your father used to say to me—that he thought I was like a skeleton?"

Papa was tall and straight with a proud bearing from his training as a Prussian officer. His face and figure resembled the former President de Gaulle of France. Dressed in the smart, gray-green police officer's uniform of high-peaked cap, calf-length greatcoat with padded shoulders, tight flared breeches and shiny black, knee-high jack boots, Jill had found him sinisterly reminiscent of the Nazi

S.S. of the long-over war. (One day when Horst put on his father's uniform for a lark, Jill became unnerved and begged him to take it off. Her beloved husband, Horst, was not a German of that evil period).

"Yool-ee-ah," Horst mimicked his father's accent. Papa always dismissed her name, Jill, as a non-name, calling her Julia instead. How her father-in-law would poke and pinch her thin arm and ask when she was going to fatten up into a strong Teutonic frau. "Julia, you must eat and fatten up or you will never bear strong sons," intoned Horst, lightly gripping her arm. "You always thought he was going to add on "for the Fatherland, didn't you?" Jill managed a weak smile.

"Poor old Jill," sighed Horst. "You never did get used to the food, did you? Well, I can tell you I was never more pleased to get back to decent food after the so-called English cuisine of unspiced meats and blankets of gravy over everything."

Yet Jill found unpalatable the assortment of strange cold sausage which came in all shapes, sizes, colours, textures, tastes and consistencies. She preferred a diet of eggs in any shape or form with a soft white bread roll—not the dark brown heavy German bread. Papa considered her cornflakes and milk non-nutritional cardboard and a liquid suitable only for babies. But, oh, those cups of coffee—freshly ground and brewed, the warm, rich aroma of which filled the early morning hours!

Papa disparaged Jill's habit of asking for a glass of water with every meal, she being unused to the abundance of delicious honey-tasting Rhein wine. How he would tut-tut, sniff and infer that water was only for washing and quenching fires—not thirst!

"You found your bete-noire there, didn't you, liebling—the terrible toilet, as you called it?" Horst jogged her elbow and her memory about the apartment plumbing in Ludwigshafen.

"Yes." Jill shuddered at the thought. "That narrow cell-like room where I either had to sing non-stop to show the place was occupied, or make a three yard dash to grab the moving handle of the unlocked door." She rattled on. "That hard seat below the overhead cistern with the long chain which dislodged whenever I tugged on it—and the tiny high up window with its useless fanning summer breezes and freezing winter blasts. And worst of all, that little ledge where everything landed for inspection before flushing. Grossed me out.

"For a moment," she continued, " I thought you were talking about the stairs, but, of course, I remember now that you never gave them a second thought having bounded up and down them for most of your life. I'd had a lifetime of two-storey houses with only one short staircase."

"Oh, those stairs! Eight steep flights of stone steps that wound from the cobbled avenue below up through the silent interior of the echoing apartment building to the family's cozy home. How her mother-in-law managed to do the tortuous ascent several times a day was beyond Jill's comprehension. Down for fresh morning rolls; to the kindergarten twice a day with her little grandson. Down for the day's bargain at the butcher for the midday meal and up again loaded with Papa's wine and beer or heavy buckets of coal from the cellar.

Those same ninety-six steps demoralized Jill. After a long bus and train trip to and from Heidelberg, twenty miles away, to her office job with the U.S. Forces, she was already exhausted before tackling the stairs to reach the sanctuary and comfort of the apartment. She felt that her father-in-law had never got over the fact that she was not the strong, blond maiden he swears Horst wrote to them about on a postcard from London, the one he had met, become engaged to and about to marry. To make matters worse, Papa was always waiting at the apartment door to observe her gasping and panting entry.

She smiled as she recalled the ruse she developed to deceive him. How she had taken her time climbing the stairs, pausing for breath on each landing and to gaze out onto the courtyard below and the balconies across the way. On arriving at the front door, she would relax, compose herself, make perfunctory repairs with comb and lipstick and then ring the bell. To her delight, when Papa opened the door, and was amazed to see that his pale, weak English daughter-in-law was not about to succumb, the smirk fell from his face.

Poor Papa! A scholar himself, upon hearing of his son's wife's scholastic achievements which included seven years of Latin, he decided to test her. He quoted Latin idiom after idiom. Yet another disappointment. She was unable to translate any of them. "Oh dear, Horst, I couldn't do anything right in your father's eyes," lamented Jill.

Now the landing with its strewn litter was flooded with memories. She hoped she hadn't sounded too complaining about her early days with her husband's family in Germany. They had, in fact, been so very kind to her. It was she who had been over-sensitive.

"Well, after so many years," she said softly, holding Horst's arm, "I think we've all grown to love and respect each other, don't you think?" He nodded, his thoughts elsewhere, as he reached for the birthday photos. Memories came alive. His round blue eyes were distant and thoughtful.

"There's so much to tell," he murmured. "Where do I start?"

Jill was pleased. She hadn't expected it to be so easy. Then noticing the book which Jill had surreptitiously brought into view, he asked, "Isn't that the famous book?"

He really was in the swing of things, thought Jill, secretly delighted. Well, no time like the present!

So, seated on the floor at the top of the stairs, surrounded by scattered photos, albums, assorted papers and magazines, two parallel stories began to unfold—Horst's story and Jill's.

Two tales seen through rose-coloured, rain-spattered spectacles. Stories of love and war, tears and laughter, families, friends and foes, a mother, a father, a brother and a chance meeting.

"Tell me your childhood before the war, liebling," she urged. He began to speak...

CHAPTER 3

"Berlin 1936! We lived upstairs on the second floor of a tall, imposing stone apartment building. I remember our cozy, little apartment and the tiny larder I'd hide in to escape from Mama's scoldings or, wrapped in a warm rubbery blanket, to daydream the moments away in the dark.

"Then downstairs I would go to play in the street with the other children. Mama always kept a lookout from the upstairs window as I was only four years old. Sometimes I would ride my tricycle that Mama would have to carry up and down the stairs from our apartment." He paused and glanced at Jill, for he knew what she was thinking.

"Your poor mother," she said right on cue, "A lifetime of climbing stairs!"

"A few houses up the street," continued Horst, "there lived an old cobbler with a big nose, peering, nervous eyes and walked with a stoop. He was like a character from Grimm's Fairy Tales. His shop was below the street level in a basement. Whenever the children crowded around the little window to watch him work, or antagonize him by blocking off his light, he would rush out muttering and chase us away.

"When I told my parents about this, they would say, "Oh, yes. That's old—I don't remember his name—the Jew with the big nose! Then to frighten me, Papa would hook his finger to his nose and croak in a menacing voice, "I'm the old Jew and I'm going to get you."

"I remember Mama then as plump, wholesome and very protective of me. My father was extremely tall, the only one in his family with such height.—a trait never attributed to any branch of the family. He looked so smart in his Prussian Police lieutenant's uniform.

"Whenever I played in the street and stayed out too long, I would hear Mama call me by my name. "Horst, Horst, kom rauf!" "Come upstairs, Horst". No nickname, always Horst."

Jill interrupted. "I can't believe that, dear. She surely called you Horstchen, just as you sometimes call me Jillchen. I love it when you call me that—Jilly or little Jill. So, little Horst, let's hear some more. Ja? He smiled and nodded.

"Opa Schaar, Mama's father, was a slim, happy-go-lucky extrovert of medium height and wavy, brown hair which he would lose in his mid-thirties. It was whispered around that he smoked and drank too much. Something not quite right there! He once peeled a banana, took a bite and handed me the rest. 'No, no, don't eat it,' I was told. Mama and Papa exchanged anxious glances and appeared to be very angry with Opa, my grandfather. I guess because he had a chronic cough, they suspected it might be contagious.

"He owned and operated an old-fashioned Berlin wirtshaft or pub. He was its best customer. His wife, my Oma or Grandma, was a short, jovial, round-faced, hardworking, strong German woman. As well as running her home, she worked day and night in the pub in order to combat the losses incurred by my grandfather. He just drank and gambled away all their profits."

"Just like in one of my grandparent stories that's coming up," mentioned Jill. "Carry on, lieb."

"Just to illustrate what a happy-go-lucky ne'er-do-well he was, I'll tell you a story Mama told me about her father. A likeable but impetuous fellow, he was once sitting in his house slippers chatting to some men friends in the pub. Talk got around to Munich and the Beer Festival going on at the time. A few drinks later and with enthusiasm at a high, Opa Schaar walked out the door just as he was and set off for Munich with his pals. The first Oma was to know of his whereabouts was a telephone call to say that he would be returning home to Berlin, an eight hour train journey away, when his money ran out! Opa Schaar died in his early fifties.

"The pub had a small restaurant as well. Oma was famous for her Bouletten, a kind of spicy hamburger. I remember the scene as if it were yesterday," Horst continued. "As an observant boy, I noticed everything around me. I can see myself standing inside the shop watching Oma, seated by the front window, mix the ingredients. People would gather around outside in the cold winters of Berlin and watch her careful preparation. As she stirred together the ground beef, onions, spices and eggs, their mouths began to water. Resisting temptation no longer, they would rush in, drooling and eager to sample the juicy, aromatic hamburgers frying in two huge black pans.

"In later years we would rather contemptuously refer to her as Die Bouletten Braterin or The Old Burger Frylady. How sad I feel when I remember the family's derisive laughter. Oma Schaar was not only a kind woman, but a clever business one as well.

"In the bitter cold winters of Berlin, even beer at room temperature was too cold to drink. Oma had an ever-ready remedy. On the huge pot-bellied stove in the center of the pub stood a large cauldron of boiling water. Foot-long metal bars one inch in circumference were placed inside..

"Whenever a customer wished to take the chill off his beer, he would pick up and place one of these hot bars into his full glass. Hey presto, in a matter of seconds, the beer became deliciously palatable."

What a clever woman, thought Jill, just like my own grandma. Horst continued as if reliving the moment. "On Sundays we visited Opan and Oma Schaefer, Papa's parents who live in another part of Berlin. A short tram ride and we are soon there, arriving at a multi-storied apartment building similar to ours. They live a few floors up. Their apartment seems immense compared to our little cozy one.

"As soon as we are greeted and embraced at the front door, I rush to the candy jar, take off the lid and reach inside for a Gummi Baerchen, fruit gums in the shape of Teddy Bears. Opa then beckons me over to his huge desk of polished wood. He sits me down at his side and brings out a book, usually an educational one with pictures. Opa was a school principal. We go through the book page by page. He smells of tobacco and schnapps. His egg-shaped head has little hair. He had the same high-bridged nose as my father.

"Oma Schaefer has always looked the same, unchanging in appearance from the time I was a small boy to when I became an adult. She always seemed about 85 years old. A small, thin, hunched up, no-neck woman with small features and scraped-back thin gray hair, she always wore long black dresses. A mild-mannered woman, she would, however, infuriate Mama, her daughter-in-law, whenever she and Opa visited us for a meal. Opa, my father and she would sit around the dining table awaiting service from Mama. Oma would sniff and mutter 'Where is the food?' Why isn't it ready?' Then she would summon Mama by knocking on the table with the handle of her knife."

Horst glanced at Jill and stopped her before she could get the words out. "I knew you'd have a quick comment to that story." He had years ago told her how his mother had longed for the day when she could retaliate with the same knife-knocking on the table to her own daughter-in-law—her son's wife, Jill, whom, she later confessed to her son, she realized was not the one to try it on!

"We lived in Berlin until 1938," continued Horst. "I had no family playmates such as cousins as I was the first grandchild of the two families. My sister was born three years later, but try as hard as I may, I cannot remember her as a child. I was possibly so full of myself. It seems I spent most of my childhood with adults, a lifelong habit acquired and since preferred.

"I remember visiting Mama's aunt, Aunt Clara, and her husband, wealthy Uncle Spielhagen. Aunt Clara had nursed her rich patient back to health and ended up marrying him. He owned and operated a lucrative factory that produced Bullrich Saltz (equivalent to Alka-Seltzer), a booming industry in a country such as Germany with its love of good eating and drinking!

"It was this uncle by marriage who had the family fortune which would, hopefully, one day seep down to us. It was a standing family joke that Papa had only married Mama for her prospective fortune. However, although Uncle died early, Aunt Clara took over the business and lived to a ripe old age enjoying extravagant living and long recuperative spells at Germany's famous spas. Now and then she would dole out piecemeal amounts to the patiently waiting beneficiaries. By 1969 when my aunt did die, although most of the beneficiaries had predeceased her, Mama then first in line received a only a pittance left over from the huge fortune."

Jill remembered how generous Mama had immediately divided up her inheritance and given a portion to each of her children, not wanting them to wait as she had done for the money to trickle down after her death.

"Uncle Spielhagen," continued Horst "was very fond of Papa. When we visited them in their expansive estate outside Berlin in the countryside, he would take him deer hunting. Being childless, too, I was especially welcome and spoiled with kindness.

"One night when Uncle and Papa had gone out to hunt, I was awakened by a noise. I crept out of bed and peered out between the banisters to see a magnificent stag. Its lolling head with blank staring eye and branching antlers trailed on the ground. It had a bullet wound in the neck. Blood seeped down onto an old canvas rug put down to protect the polished floor.

"One night Mama wanted to join in the hunt. I refused to let her leave my room as I was frightened to be left alone, though more likely, I was jealous because I could not join in the hunt. I remember tears of sorrow running down Mama's face as she slowly shook her head from side to side. Her four year old son was a tyrant who had chained her to the chair in his bedroom!

Jill listened, entranced. "That's marvelous, mein Liebling. You certainly have a good memory. You'd better take a breather and let me tell about my grandparents, though I doubt I can top that stag story! She opened the book, found the page and began to read...

CHAPTER 4

"England—early 1900 onwards." Jill paused to pick up a pair of 8x10 studio photo portraits of Grandma and Grandpa Field, a larger-than-life couple, her mother's parents.

"Their seven children, four girls (of whom Mother was the oldest) and three boys were their pride and joy. Grandma and Grandpa were the talk and envy of all. The entire neighbourhood admired these seven little Fields when dressed in flouncy dresses with big bows atop the girls' curls and the boys in smart sailor suits, as they took their daily airings strutting along a la crocodile with their nursery maid.

"Those Fields of beauty and bounce were the First Family of Fulham, the saints of the Parish Church and the stars of the local tennis club. Ivy Field, nee Stoneham, at age twenty-three married her employer, Thomas Field, a bachelor of forty and owner of several off-licence stores. His parents, millers from Gloucestershire, who had despaired that he would never marry, were delighted when he did. Grandma, of the brown eyes and long reddish hair—inherited as yet by only four of her more than sixty descendants—was slim when married. Seven births in almost as many years transformed her into a stocky, big-boned, bosomy woman with a determined square jaw. She became a clever business woman and the matriarch of her vast family, their spouses and their children.

"Jill interrupted her reading. "'I have a lock of Grandma's hair that Grandpa cut off and entwined with an ivy leaf. The silky fine strands are strawberry blond, not at all the redhead I'd been led to believe.'

"They would in later years through her diabetic condition and over-indulgence of all the black market delicacies of wartime England weigh well over nineteen stone, about 270 lbs. 'Work it out yourself in kilos, lieb. I've no idea,' she added. "She died at the young age of sixty-seven in her daughter Ivy's London home. She had spent ten years of widowhood living with each of two daughters, Mother and Bibby (who both had downstairs abodes along with the compassion and patience to care for her).

Jill confided to Horst. "When Grandma died, the nurse and Mother were unable to turn her over for the laying out. So they sought out Father's help, who pale and quaking fortified himself with a stiff shot of brandy before and after the ordeal. He'd never been able to stand doctors, disease or death in any shape or form!" She continued reading.

"The Field's first family home was in a many-roomed terraced house in Hammersmith, a West London suburb. Their next and final home was in the two-storey dwelling above the off-licence in Fulham, five miles away in a busy, noisy street market.

"Ramshackle wooden stalls laden with an assortment of wares from live quacking ducks to delicate shiny-smooth linens, lined each side of the narrow main street. Motor cars, buses and horse-drawn coal and milk carts crushed close to each other among the smelly garbage and strewn-about litter. The raucous unintelligible cockney cries of costermongers, garbed in tatty overcoats and cloth caps could be heard above the din. Barrow-women with metal curlers peeping out over one eye beneath a greasy headscarf rubbed their chapped fingers, red from exposure to the chilly dampness of soggy lettuces and dirty root vegetables. The Black Market 'spiv' barrow-boys quickly hid away their illicit loot from the eye of the approaching arm of the law.

"Between the curb-hugging barrows and shop-front door with its tinkling bell was a large covered square hole in the pavement through which the beer barrels were hoisted down by rope into the dark cellar below stacked full with crates. Left in their wake was a pool of seeped-out foam and dark pools of pungent-smelling hops, refreshed anew with each delivery.

"It is this abode that I remember with great love. It was here that I played with my brothers in the grimy back yard among the piles of towering empty crates that were our kingdom castles and golden carriages of childhood play.

"It was here in this house, that we children riding high on sturdy shoulders would go up the wooden hill to bed to snuggle up warm, cozy and safe. It was here under the huge dining table, laden with enormous quantities of food (the Fields liked to eat), that we would sit among the adult legs and listen to the indignant murmurings of wartime deeds along with the laughter and gossip of family loves and strife.

"It was here that huge, lurching Uncle Charlie, the only remaining son, with the boozy beer breath, would swing me up to the ceiling and across the walls upon which hung a black and white framed print 'The Pride of the Lions'. For many years I thought the lioness was the animal with the big mane of hair a la Fields and curly fashion of the Thirties and Forties.

"Grandpa Field" –'I always love to tell this,' would surprise us with huge fat pencils packed with thick black lead and engraved with the Field Stores inscription. We would proudly take them to our kindergarten where I remember crying so bitterly on my first day away from Mother.

"The upstairs rooms were sinister and hold unpleasant remembrances of being clutched fast asleep from my bed beneath the window when the pane of glass shattered into tiny fragments all over me. It was the blast from a nearby exploding bomb, a direct hit on either the Power Station or one of the munitions factories coveted by the German bombers during World War II. Almost as bad was that I had to sleep in Grandma's bed with its icy sheets next to huge cushiony Grandma wearing an immense crisp-crackling nightgown.

"In a little side bedroom Grandpa, aged 75 and considered terribly old by his young daughters, lay on his death bed. I remember being taken up to see him and told to feel the space under the covers where the doctors had cut off his gangrenous limb to save him from certain death! The feel of that empty space still chills me. I can still see his dear kind whiskery face and hear his gruff voice saying, as he stroked my head, 'Don't frighten the child.'

"You know, Horst," said Jill thoughtfully. "I found out years later that it was only on his death bed that Grandpa converted to Catholicism, much against his will. But Grandma, the only convert in a staunchly Protestant family, badgered her husband during his lifetime to become a Catholic. She managed to do it only when he finally gave in to the priest in attendance at his bedside."

"Of the three sons, two were already dead, leaving the white-headed Charlie who had few years left to him. Clifford, the darling baby of the seven—a dear, sweet fair-haired angel of a boy, adored by all his siblings—died of pneumonia at age fifteen. An ardent boy scout, he had returned home from an outing drenched to the skin from a sudden downpour. He remained in his damp clothes and developed a cold which worsened into pneumonia that led to his untimely death. (A victim of his time, I fear. With the magical medicines and antibiotics of later decades, he surely would have survived.) Mother, (unable to attend his funeral owing to a sudden illness) was devastated and never forgot the tragedy. Hence her urgent warnings to my older brother, Peter, a stalwart and keen boy scout himself for many a year, to never remain in wet clothes or disregard the slightest sniffle.

"Tom, or Sonny as he was called, the oldest of the seven, was the bright, clever son who was to inherit the business. I did hear, though, that he was directly responsible for the Fulham off-licence losing money. That put his parents into debt and forced them to relinquish the business to their oldest son, Tom! As fate would have it, Tom also met an untimely death in the downstairs shop from a fall off a ladder leaning against the shelves laden with bottles of liquor. Only in his early thirties, he was at the time engaged to our enchanting, fashionably dressed 'Auntie' Queenie, who with her long red-lacquered fingernails would thrill me with spine-tingling tickles down my arm. On weekends, she would take me to the cemetery where, as she tended and tidied his grave, I would reach up and pick the fruit off the only crab apple tree in the whole of London! She never married, but remained our auntie, long mourning Sonny until her own death"

Jill turned the page to find a picture of her other grandmother, her father's mother. "It's not a very good photo," she murmured "though the chimney pots silhouetted against the gray sky do give an artistic touch. In fact, I wrote this in the book. 'Until the Smokeless Air Act of somewhere in the late Fifties or early Sixties, I remember all those chimneys belching from October to April choking black smoke and grime. What a difference the use of smokeless fuel and the introduction of central heating, both gas and oil, made to the murky skies of London.'

"And," she chuckled, "how indignant I became when hearing the only comment a stranger could dream up to start a friendly conversation and identify with my country and me, was—yes, you know, Horst—Foggy London." Horst cleared his throat self-consciously for he had been guilty of it on their first meeting.

"Even the old Hollywood movies unfailingly opened with the swirling fogs of dark, crime-ridden London streets, as undoubtedly it used to be long ago. She turned to Horst. "Well, shall I continue reading about Grandma Martin and my father's side of the family, or do you want another turn?"

Without replying, he adjusted his position on the floor to make himself more comfortable, and then began to speak. Jill's reminiscences had revived many of his own memories.

CHAPTER 5

"Look at this," Horst began, fingering a photo by his side. "Berlin 1937/38! I remember Himmler's elite Storm troopers marching down the wide street outside our apartment building. Towering above me, how smart and well-dressed they were in their brown uniforms and polished knee-high black boots. As they goose-stepped in unison—plonk, plonk—their pointed toes snapped high above my head and back down to the echoing cobblestones. How thrilling it was! They marched in formation four abreast with the final six to eight men in couples on either side. This left a space in the middle that made the column appear longer. It was inside this corridor that we children would run, march and sing, and moved along with the troopers as if inside a traveling fortress.

"One day when I returned home from kindergarten, I went into the kitchen and saw Mama sitting at the table crying. Papa was pacing up and down anxiously, his hands folded behind his back. In front of Mama lay a letter from Police Headquarters, informing them that Papa was to be transferred from Berlin to a town further south called Ludwigshafen.

"I learned later that this was part of Hitler's plan to integrate Germany by implanting officers of Prussian stock, such as Papa, among the more southerly peasant areas. In exchange police officers from those regions were transferred to Berlin. It was Hitler's hope that the elite Prussians would elevate their inferiors through example and education. This plan was Hitler's attempt to freshen up the blood.

"Mama and Papa didn't even know where Ludwigshafen was. When they looked at a map of Germany, they found a tiny village of about 500 inhabitants situated in the deep south of Germany on Lake Constance, Bodensee, just across the border from Switzerland. They were desolate to leave their beloved Berlin, the city of their birth and their parents, too.

"It turned out, however, that Papa was to be transferred to another Ludwigshafen on the River Rhein in the southwest of Germany close to the French border. Mannheim, across the river, is its twin city. At least knowing that it was a city and not quite so far away made the parting from their beloved Berlin less painful.

The furniture men came and picked up all our belongings which were taken away in a large van. Mama, Papa, my little sister and I traveled by express train to Mannheim where we moved into a small apartment in another large building.

"I was never able to go up the wooden hill to bed, as you do in England.. The only stairs were the flights of stone steps outside the front door to the street below or those inside the building. In Germany everyone is sent to Bettenhauesen where all good German children sleep peacefully in beds shaped like houses in a place called Bedland. We started school in 1939.

"One morning Papa said to me, 'You may go to school two hours late today. Our beloved Chancellor, Adolf Hitler, is going to make a speech on the radio and I want you to stay and listen.

"I knew Papa would expect a detailed report from me, so I sat down and concentrated with my ear close to the big radio. I remember he said something about how Germany and its people must become stronger in order to defend themselves. Then he went on to say how unjust it was that Germany had such a small navy.

"I clung onto those words, repeating them over and over until I could report them intelligently to Papa. The rest of the speech was somewhat garbled and strident. When Hitler concluded, I applauded. The window was wide open for all the neighbours to hear."

Horst paused momentarily to take a quick breath and continued with hardly a pause. "A tall for my age, blue-eyed young boy with light brown hair and just out of kindergarten, how I enjoyed Sunday mornings in our Ludwigshafen home. I would creep into Mama and Papa's huge bed, crawl into the middle and snuggle up between them. Wrapped in their warm-smelling cover, it was time for our Sunday morning chat."

Jill remembered similar Sunday mornings with her own parents. How she and her brothers would love to jump up and down on the springy mattress when her parents went downstairs for a quiet breakfast. The thump, thump, thump on the ceiling below usually got an angry call from her father. She quickly turned her attention back to Horst who was still talking and listened to his story.

"Papa and I were the men of the family and we'd side against Mama. Although my sister was there, I only remember Papa and me.

"Horst," Papa would say. 'We are the men and are flying high in a golden airplane. Your mother is down below,' he added scornfully, pointing down. 'Up there we will have fine meals and perhaps maybe throw a crumb to your mother.' He looked proudly at me and snidely at Mama. In hindsight, I realize that the smile on Mama's face was more pained than pleased. She never counter-attacked, although I am sure she was hurt.

"Having put me in such an exalted position, Papa would then ask me 'Well, Horst, where would you rather be? With me in the golden plane or down below picking up crumbs with your mother?' Naturally I preferred being up in the plane. It was more manly and exciting. However, I felt guilty and decided to let Mama know that I would rather be with her picking up the crumbs. At the time I was too cowardly to side with Mama, who, although being my mother, was only a mere woman. And I had to prove myself as a man before being accepted into the Adolf Hitler school.

Jill felt sorry for the young mother of long ago. She knew that her own mother would never have stood for such teasing. It just goes to show the difference in upbringing, countries and culture and, to a large extent, social and economic standing, she thought.

"I notice, my dear Horst, that you've never tried telling me such a teasing story," she bantered.

"No, you would never have put up with it, so I never tried," he replied, turning the page of Jill's book. Pointing to two photos in a magazine, he said, 'I didn't know, liebling, that you'd been in print before our newspaper engagement article. That is you, isn't it?'

Jill had almost forgotten the two black and white photographs, part of an educational article in Goodhousekeeping magazine—July 1941, in which Mother and her three children made their modeling debuts.

"The first one," Jill explained "portrays a charming domestic scene in which a slim, pretty blond woman poised on the edge of an armchair is reading to her three children. The older child, my nine year old brother, Peter, dressed in crisp school gray and seated on a pouffe, is listening intently with chin in cupped hands. The little girl, me, aged, 6, demure in bright floral, puff-sleeved cotton dress (which to my sorrow would fade and become limp from repeated washings), has shiny brown bobbed straight hair. She is squatting on the floor at her brother's feet. The plump, contented year-old baby was Mother's 'easy' child. How proud she was of his huge fatness as he sat smiling and immobile on the floor. This is my younger brother, Mike, or Junior as he was called, being Father's thirty-third birthday present from Mother. Fourteen years later Mike would put his foot down and refuse to answer anymore to the juvenile nickname.

In the picture he is leaning against Mother and pointing to the book she is reading.

"Poor Mother, only 34 years old, whom I sacrificed to die at the hands of the wicked Germans instead of me. The difficult choice of who would I choose was put to me by a playmate during one of our long philosophical walks home from school. After a lot of rationalization in my six year old mind I came up with the answer. It was quite simple. Mother had lived her life and I had all mine before me!

"It was the time of The Last War (as it was euphemistically called until renamed The Second World War or World War II by a later generation who knew by then that it was a misnomer). Mother always boasted that none of her four children were 'war babies'. We three in the picture were born before its outbreak and my youngest brother, Christopher, was delivered in the peacetime of 1945.

The blacks, white and grays of the old photos reminded Jill of the gray days of wartime England; silent facades to colourful memories. She recited a story told her by her mother.

"The only war-related death in the family happened, I remember, to one of my Grandma Field's three brothers, a man in his sixties. Shell-shocked and terrified of the bombs, he always had to be escorted home. One dreadful night during an air-raid he had to make his way home alone and was in such a nervous state on his arrival that he tried to commit suicide by drinking prussic acid. The burning pain was so intense that he got a razor and cut his throat." She grimaced and turned back to her book. "Listen, Horst, to what I wrote here about the war.

"The blackish blue skies appeared bruised from the ghostly apparitions of the silver barrage balloons tethered to the ground below as they float aloft to ward off the deadly Messerschmitt enemy planes. The pointed shadows of death silently bore down towards the helpless mass of humanity below; some were abed in the dank spidery underground shelters amid the Victory vegetable gardens; others huddled in winter coats over night-wear beneath the stairs or deep underground on the platforms of the railway stations. Faces were strained and fingers crossed to ward off the death and destruction hurtling towards them.

"As the incendiary bomb plopped onto the roof, it explodes into red, orange and blue-white flames, and sputters a while as if discontented with its landing; then to burst erratically into a sparkling firework display to entertain no-one but the air-raid wardens who douse its beauty and danger with water aimed from a hastily uncoiled hose and buckets of bright yellow sand."

Horst looked somewhat bemused at his wife's dramatic recitation.

"Well, let me finish up the story about the magazine picture. Okay? she pleaded.

"Following our minor success as models in the Goodhousekeeping magazine, a neighbour of ours, a photographer with a bushy beard, stopped by to visit my parents. Very suspect were beards in those days unless one was a sailor home on leave or a foreign spy a la Mr. Funk in Tommy Handley's wartime comic I.T.M.A (It's That Man Again) show on the radio. This was a Sunday never to be missed midday programme, listened to around the family roast dinner and followed by the Forces Favourites top tune record show.

"Well this bearded neighbour engaged our time and talent in exchange for which Mother received a little pin money. We also modeled for knitting pattern covers and kept the outfits--manna from heaven during the days of clothes rationing. The photographer's success was as fleeting as our own for he spent the rest of the war in prison as a conscientious objector!"

Jill lay down the book and stretched her arms. Horst should really have another turn, she thought, if he's ready with anything to say. "A cuppa would go down well, wouldn't it." she asked. Horst made no reply for he was reaching for another picture.

CHAPTER 6

"Oh, that one," said Jill, looking at the tiny photo. "I'm going to look like this grandmother when I get old. We have the same long face, elegant nose and tall, slim build. Don't you think so, Horst? Without waiting for a reply, she began to read.

"Grandma Martin, my father's mother, had long bony limbs which I never saw as they were always hidden beneath an ankle-length black skirt. I have the same slim fingers with Filbert nails which Mother encouraged me to keep strong and healthy by dosing me with calcium.

"Grandma's hair, as I've been told, was wispy-fine straight and nondescript brown, just like mine. Father remembers when he was a young boy her hair was waist length and how he enjoyed combing it. In this photo her hair is gray and dragged back into a puny bun, as I remember it. Mother always used to say—and I intend following suit—Old may I get, but gray, never!' She kept her word. Would that I had a combination of both my grandmothers' hair—reddish brown chestnut with thick, glossy curls. Many, undoubtedly, have noticed over the years my repeated attempts to achieve it," she said, glancing over at her husband He laughed. "So that's why you haven't any gray hair like me. You've been disguising it, haven't you, lieb," he teased. Jill ignored him and continued reading.

"Father inherited his mother's hair. When he became almost bald in his late twenties, he would complain that I had stolen his hair. It was a joke that united us for a brief moment as father and daughter.

"Grandma Martin, as we called her to distinguish her from Mother's mother, Grandma Field—as different from each other as chalk from cheese—had nine children. Somewhere in the family were triplets, a girl and two boys. She breastfed the two boys, who died, and bottle fed the girl, who survived. We never knew Grandma Martin's husband, so we never called him Grandpa. He died when Father was twelve years old. No photos have been found. I've made a study of the family distinguishing traits and traced them back to living family members or old photographs and thus was able to form a composite picture of this grandfather. So far he has a short upper lip, my older brother's distinctive nose and a small, square head with a slight build and not overly tall.

"None of Father's eight siblings ever had a kind word to say about their this grandfather. Even Father, after much probing, confided that his father had at one time deserted the family to gamble away all their money and returned to sire a total of nine children. As was customary in Catholic families of the early 1900s, a child was born every year, even though his wife, a devout woman, I'm told, said 'never on Sundays'. I do know that he held a clerical job at Hammersmith Town Hall and was a hard taskmaster. It was a time of harsh discipline and chastisement for the family. Father remembers being cared for in infancy by his older sisters, Grandma presumably either being too ill or busy. Father's boyhood was spent for the most part up a tree, escaping his father's wrath and cane!

"I must have seen that tree many a time on our father-daughter visits to Grandma. How I delighted in the old-fashioned lavender scent of her home full of shiny trinkets, mechanical music boxes and pure white lace doilies daintily placed on the arms and backs of the over-stuffed armchairs.

"What a housekeeper! A trait she passed on to Father who would follow me around on my Saturday morning chores as my brother and I cleaned all the copper and brass. He would check on the shine of the brass ornaments and the dust left on the sideboard, deducting from our pocket money for each speck discovered!

"My Auntie May, one of Father's older sisters, also inherited the same trait. Whenever she visited our home, she would infuriate Mother as this aunt slid her finger along the furniture and mantelpiece to collect the dust. Then, she would silently hold aloft the smudged finger tip for all to see. A good housekeeper Mother was not. Bright and cheery was her home, but never clean enough in the eyes of those Martin-in-laws! I became a mixture of both, delighting in a clean, tidy home, but hating to do it!

"Ah, so, Jill," said Horst. "How right you are. You certainly know yourself well." He remember to himself how dismayed his own mother who kept an impeccable German household, had been to see his new wife's lackadaisical housekeeping. Jill interrupted his thoughts.

"I know what you're thinking. But I can tell you that when I first saw German housewives cleaning their windows at seven in the morning and airing their bedclothes on the window sills until noon every day, well, I decided once and for all that I was in no way going to compete with such industriousness!"

"No complaints, liebling. None at all," he said hastily. "Carry on reading. I'm waiting for my turn."

"Well, here's where I tell about Auntie May and" she continued reading "our family musical gatherings when Mother would endeavour to accompany on the baby grand. She wasn't at all bad but certainly not the concert pianist she dreamed of being, a la Eileen Joyce, who was then at her peak. Mother delivered a fairly good rendition of 'The Warsaw Concerto', far better than Father's effort of his one and only repertoire of 'In A Monastery Garden'. This he plonked out flatly with his large-knuckled nicotine-stained fingers as they sprawled across the wrong notes of the flowing runs. Then it was the turn of Auntie May and her little Welsh husband, Uncle Bob. We had to endure the discordant wailings of their duet, with a hand-wringing, floor-kneeling, eye-wiping performance and an unasked-for encore. My brother, Peter, and I both ended with songs--his reluctant rendition of 'I Took my Harp to a Party (and nobody asked me to play), and my 'Sweet Little Alice Blue Gown', both followed by enthusiastic applause. Fortunately no-one asked for an encore. Just as well as mortified Peter had fled the scene.

"Auntie Edie, another older sister, was the only unmarried one. Not that she hadn't had her chances, as she would later confide to me. She lived with her mother until Grandma died and then continuing her solitary life which she apparently enjoyed, as she was an avid reader and forever refused the offer of a television. Auntie Edie, with the small head, lean frame and large round, heavy-lidded eyes which I shall put atop Grandpa Martin's nose and upper lip.

"When Grandma Martin died I happened to be on a three months leave of absence from my secretarial job in California and was back home in London. I was almost twenty-two and she was in her mid eighties. I remember borrowing Mother's black moleskin fur coat to keep me warm and suitably funereal as we gathered around her grave on a freezing November day.

"I still have the exercise book with the torn blue cover which Auntie Edie gave me when I was questing for remembrances. Grandma's inscription on the front cover 'Mary M. Martin' in her spidery handwriting, the same as Father's. Her old scrapbook contains cuttings of reflective poems, religious articles and her own composition written in pen and ink entitled 'The Rosary'. Very devout was Grandma Martin, as was the whole family. She even had an aunt who was a nun. But she was possibly full of doubts too. How torn she must have been between duty to her marriage and protection of her self, when after so many loveless years of childbearing, she barred her unloved husband from her bed!"

Jill closed the book and thought for a moment. "That reminds me. My middle names were Mary and Ivy, from my two grandmothers. Now, whereas my three brothers all had saints names, I, the only girl, was named after a London West End musical 'Jill Darling'. Guess I wasn't deserving of a saint's name!" She laughed. "As for my name, I tried to change it. I wanted a popular nickname, so I put together JIM for Jill Ivy Martin but it never took off. How I longed to hear 'Jim' from across the crowded classroom or shouted loud and clear to pass the ball across the hockey field."

"Well, there you have it, my dear. I love it when you call me Jillchen. And your name, Horst. Didn't you say it means an eagle's nest? He nodded. "How romantic! And to think Mother has never been able to pronounce the 't' and calls you Horse!

CHAPTER 7

With a good imitation of a horse whinnying, Horst requested that he have a turn. He had a lot to say. "I will not say 'neigh'," replied his wife, with a laugh. "No horsing around, mind you. Just get on with it." This he did.

"Ludwigshafen," he said, on pointing to a photo of his father who had become a police captain. "His uniform was quite different from the one he wore in Berlin. Now it was gray-green with a high-peaked cap, knee-high black jack boots and a long, heavy winter coat with shoulder pads."

He glanced over at Jill. He could tell by the expression on her face that there was no need to remind her of her alarm on her arrival in Germany after their wedding to meet his father clad in the uniform so reminiscent of the Nazi Secret Service police. And then when he himself later tried on the uniform, how his father insisted that Horst reassure his young wife that times were different. The wartime days of the Germany-England conflict were long gone by.

"Papa was entrusted with civil and air defence in Ludwigshafen," continued Horst. His job involved the organization of material, such as concrete, for the construction of the large bunkers being built throughout the city. The structures were windowless, cone-shaped, six-storey high air-raid shelters. Each had a roof and looked like any ordinary apartment building from the searching enemy bombers in the sky above.

"At the time of their construction it appeared rather a useless plan. Yet, we had no idea how valuable they would be in the very near future as life-saving buildings.

"In 1941 Opa and Oma Schaefer came to visit us for Christmas. Opa was a life-long socialist and he and Papa would have heated discussions on the present Nazi socialistic system. Papa was idealistic about Hitler's regime which, in his opinion, promised an orderly, peaceful existence for the German people. Opa was more realistic and could see the writing on the wall!

"Whenever they had their heated discussions they always made sure the windows were closed and that there were no strangers in the apartment, for Opa was a convinced socialist and against the Nazis. Papa would tell him to guard his words. 'They're going to get you—and me.' We children were told not to pay any attention to their talks and not to tell anyone about Papa's meetings with his father. They were most likely above suspicion for as Papa had advanced in the police force, he'd had to prove that both he and Mama were of good Aryan stock.

"Papa was a tall, imposing man well over six feet, with a large egg-shaped head, high-bridged nose and thinning brown hair. He must have cut a fine figure of a young officer who, a shy and reticent loner, met Mama, seven years his junior, when she worked in her father's pub. This was Berlin of the mid Thirties. Knowing a good catch when they saw one, both my grandfather, the hard-drinking, womanizing, extrovert innkeeper and my grandmother, the hamburger fryer, encouraged their daughter. Mama, short and comely, vivacious and sensually alert, soon chatted up and charmed the young officer, both educated and a gentleman. 'Give him a good plateful, Gerda,' Oma said encouragingly.

"Married shortly afterwards, it was and has been a happy union. They celebrated their Golden Wedding, 50 years, in 1982. The two complemented each other well, Mama in her desire to please and be appreciated and Papa in his need to be the recipient of her abundant love and service. Although Papa was the head of the family in name, it was Mama who, with MY help,' stressed Horst, 'took hold of the reins during and after the war, never again to relinquish them!

"Idealist Papa joined the Nazi party. Even if he'd had any qualms about joining, he had no other choice. It was either join or suffer the consequences. If you didn't join, it automatically implied that you were against the Party. I still have Papa's membership book.

"It was compulsory," continued Horst, "for every family to have a picture of Adolf Hitler on show in the home. A current joke was, 'Shall we hang him up or shall we stand him against the wall…?'

"On the radio On/Off button was stuck an official Nazi party sticker with the words 'It is forbidden to listen to foreign stations.' Anyone caught would immediately be sent away to a concentration camp. However, Papa would often listen to the British Broadcasting Company, the BBC, from London with its boom, boom-boom BOOM kettle-drum code signal. The Hitler Youth were encouraged to inform on such activities. Yet nobody would ever have expected me to say anything about Papa, even if I'd wanted to, for he was in a position of great trust and above suspicion.

"We had moved to a better street in Ludwigshafen and into a larger apartment that would be our home for the next thirty-seven years

"Until after the war when smaller, more attractive apartment buildings cropped up wherever there was an unbuilt-on bomb site, at that time the buildings were huge, towering stone constructions. Strangers to Germany often considered them grim, forbidding fortresses, the windows at night unseeing behind shutters and by day bedecked with white lace curtains and flowering plants. I had never known any other abode, so our many-roomed apartment with its tiny balconies and eight flights of stone stairs was a warm family home to me.

"Next door to us was an old-fashioned school building with a large concrete playground extending out to our cobbled, tree-lined street. This was my school for the next few years. Later on after the war, this building which miraculously survived the extensive bombing raids that flattened Ludwigshafen, became a barracks for the occupying American Forces.

"There's a story I remember about the school playground. I can laugh about it now, but at the time it was a stupid thing to do. American soldiers would sit on the low wall of the school yard and whenever I passed by they would yell out, 'You know fraulein who' wink and signs? We have coffee!' I was then in my early teens. Papa was a P.O.W. in France and food was scarce. In fact, whenever the troops were cooking in their field kitchen in the yard, they were always surrounded by about fifty of so of us children who held out tin plates and begged for a handout.

"After repeated solicitations by the soldiers, one day I answered boldly, 'O.K. I want two pounds of coffee, chewing gum and powdered soup.' I pointed upstairs to our apartment. Mama was entertaining a neighbour when I entered with the soldiers. She was furious. They turned and left, leaving behind the goods in their rush to put distance between them and Mama's fury!

Jill turned to Horst, astonishment on her face. I bet your father never heard that story, eh?"

"What was the point in telling him. He had enough problems when he was finally released and came home," he replied. "Anyhow, to continue with the school days.

"Athletics was a very important non-academic subject and we were trained with the Jungfolk in mind, the pre-stage to the Hitler Youth. Twice a week during afternoons we'd assembled to watch the Jungfolk groups parade around the school yard. We were told by our teachers that if we kept up our grades, were disciplined students, did well in sports and followed the Nazi doctrine, that we would be allowed to join the Jungfolk at age ten."

"Gracious me," interrupted Jill. "Peter and I had nothing like that to join, only the Cubs and Brownies and then on to the Boy Scouts and the Girl Guides."

"However," said Horst, picking up his story, "when I did get to join, I once again tyrannized Mama by refusing to attend the meetings until I got my official dagger. There was a shortage of them at the time. I also made her cut holes in the uniform shirt so I could wear a pair of braces underneath to hold my trousers up. My belt just didn't do the trick. I must have been too thin!

"How proudly I remember taking home my first school report with very passable grades. I had a lot to live up to with a school-teacher grandfather and Papa, a lover of education and learning.

"The school report was a thin book with a large black swastika on the outside cover. Inside were the words 'Halt dein Blut rein'—'Keep your blood pure' referring to the pure Aryan race Hitler was attempting to establish by annihilating less, inferior beings. Then came a quotation from Adolf Hitler's famous directive 'Mein Kampf'. The whole page looked very impressive.

Jill rummaged in her pocket and withdrew the booklet, watching delightedly as Horst's jaw dropped in astonishment.

"You found that up there? I thought it safe at home," he gasped, tenderly grasping hold of the memento.

"Well, it was suitably buried under the dust," answered Jill mischievously. "I found this, too" She waved a little Union Jack under his nose. "Talking about patriotism, I waved this flag at Empire Day celebrations in the school playground." She turned the pages of her book with the stick. "It will make a good bookmark now."

As she inserted it between the pages, a tiny black and white photo of Auntie Bibbie's, one of Mother's four sisters, wedding to Uncle Jack fell to the floor. She picked it up and chuckled at the little bridesmaid tripping down the steps behind the bride and groom. "That's me," she explained. "Thin and frail after a bout of whooping cough—or was it after Peter and I had the measles and chicken pox? Anyway, I do remember that Mother had a wartime clerical job and Father was out of work, or was manning the anti-aircraft gun for the Home Guard --and we were minded by Mrs. Leo, an Irish woman with gun-metal frizzy hair and the overpowering stale smell of the great unwashed, who, of all things," she added indignantly, "allowed her ever-hungry son to come in and raid Mother's larder on his way home from school!"

"Ah, wait, though. I remember now. It was after going to hospital to have my tonsils out. And where, of all things, I was put in an adult ward to recover. I can tell you that the sick old ladies and the over-worked nurses dreaded Mother's visits because when she left, almost in tears herself, I'd bawl my heart out!

"What a joyous home-coming it was, Horst. Mother gave me the best home-coming of all. Look it's all written down here." She pointed to a paragraph and read. "Sore of throat, small and cozy in Mother's arms after a bewildering taxi ride home, I entered the living room, bright and cheery from a coal fire, to see before me a wondrous scene of familiar faces all lined up on the sofa to greet me—Regal Porcelain Rosemary, Russian Olga with the real flaxen braids, Baby Wettums, Teddy and Golly—all my darling dolls, propped up silently shrieking their 'Welcome Home' greeting as they awaited my love and attention."

"Bear with me, lieb," she pleaded with her husband. "Listen to this other doll story." She passed him a photo showing the head and shoulders of the same little girl, a year or two older, with short brown fringe topped by a Snow White bow and a neat sausage curl framing each cheek. "This is also one of my modeling photos for a knitting book." She pointed to the intricately made twin set the smiling girl was wearing. "Such a little girl, I remember," she read "me, standing in our living room dwarfed by the furniture as my eyes darted up, down and around, craning her neck to find what Father had hidden. 'Where is it, Daddy? I can't see it! Please tell me.'

"But Father continued to play his game as he stood by the door with a smug smile on his face. 'Warm, warmer. You're getting warmer. No, cold, colder' as I moved bewilderedly in the wrong direction. Then with an impatient sigh he turned me around and raised my face towards the large radio with its tapestry Gothic arch-shaped front. 'Look up there,' he said. Suddenly I saw on the sideboard leaning against the side of the radio, a beautifully-dressed little girl doll with thick chestnut curls, a polite smile and thick, long eyelashes half-closed over blank blue eyes. 'Isn't she beautiful?' asked Father. 'Would you like to have her?' As I mutely nodded my head, he handed the beautiful doll to me."

And, added Jill, in a mysterious tone of voice, "More than a decade later he would ask me to admire yet another beautiful doll."

"What do you mean by that, Jill?" demanded Horst.

"You'll see," she replied. "Tell me about yourself at that age." Horst knew she had deliberately changed the subject.

CHAPTER 8

"While I'm thinking," said Horst, handing Jill an open magazine and pointing to the picture beneath the story-time one of Mother and her three young children. "What's this all about—another one of your fashion stints with the conscientious objector?"

"Yes, so it is," replied Jill, recognizing the two delightful children, a brother and sister, hand-in-hand on their way to school. "That's Peter in his school uniform and me in my Panama hat and floral dress, and we're both carrying our gasmasks neatly boxed and ready for use." They look picture-book happy!

"Peter, hold your sister's hand all the way to school. You're her big brother. Take care of your little sister, and if you run off again, your father will hear about it when he gets home," warned Mother.

"It was a long walk to school from our little house on the corner. The dark green front door numbered 369 with a lion-heads knocker and letter-box slit faced onto the busy road. A steady flow of red double-decker trolley buses purred by as they crackled their way along the sparking overhead rails from the underground station down to the rowdy Red Lion pub. Once there they swooshed and swayed round the corner out of sight on their way to squalid Shepherds Bush, a west London suburb.

"Sometimes Mother would pop next door to make an urgent purchase from Mr. And Mrs. Higgins, the roly-poly Happy Family card game characters and proprietors of Higgins Grocery store. Otherwise, she would rush up the wooden hill to stand vigil at the floor to ceiling Gothic window of our bedroom, from where she had an uninterrupted view of the entire length of the road. Once we reached the pub on the corner, Peter and I would turn with the buses, cross over to the top of Rylett Road at the Belisha Beacon crossing with its orange ball atop a pole and disappear from her sight. We were on the last lap to our parochial school, St. Stephens, at the bottom of the dead-ending road where we were two of the better class pupils among a sea of Irish Catholic with runny noses and a lilting brogue. The rest of the pupils were the working class poor of Shepherds Bush with their Cockney accents and rough manner.

"As we ran the length of the long road down to the school, Peter dropped my hand from his cruel clutch to dash off to find his friends. Not at all did he want to be seen with his little sister, let alone holding her hand! It was bad enough, too, that as a 'smartie' I had quickly moved up to his grade where he had to endure my presence in his classroom. No wonder he scornfully refused my help—that useless younger sister showing him up again--one day in the playground when I rushed in to rescue him from some bullies.

"Thrown together since our inception, we were the first two of the large family flock; a tempestuous team of two that divided only when we entered our one-sex high schools. Even then, though separate, we continued our academic rivalry for many years, until he drew way ahead. In later life he would become the greatest achiever of us all in his chosen field.

"By nature a loner, he carefully selected friends who complemented his individual interests and skills in outdoor sports and scouting, when not spending hours engrossed in his drawing and model-making. Such exquisitely-made galleons, ocean liners and every type of airplane adorned his room, all constructed from balsa wood and glue (plastics being unknown).

"Peter was often at loggerheads with Father who misunderstood his disrespectful, mischievous first born. Often I would see Father fuming and threatening to give him a thick ear if and when he caught him. Impish Peter would outrun him round the vegetable patch, an impudent grin on his face, as Father reached for the cane that hung in a corner of the living room, idly collecting dust! The conflict between her husband and her oldest boy, a breech baby at birth, upset Mother whom she had to admit had been a difficult child for young, first-time parents to practise on!"

Jill paused. "That reminds me, Horst. Mother had a lot of guilt over my brother. After his birth she breastfed him, as was the wont in those days. He'd feed a little, stop exhausted, sleep again only to wake up shortly to non-stop screaming. Mother wanted to bottle-feed him, but that was a no-no. She persisted week after week. Peter screamed on. Finally Mother in desperation sneaked him a full bottle of cow's milk, which he gobbled down greedily, fell asleep and on awakening became a quiet, contented baby from then on. He'd been starving!"

Horst chortled. "I like the bit about your father chasing him around the garden, too!"

"In the back of my mind," mused Jill, "I see a very clear picture of Peter on one side of the vegetable patch and a group of people the other side. My father was there, my mother and her sister, Evelyn, with her husband, Sydney (the ones we were evacuated to in the war). The two men were trying to catch Peter. My uncle wanted to give him an enema with a sliver of soap!

"No wonder Peter's running away. I would too," declared Horst. "Did they catch him? And what's this about evacuation?" Jill muttered that she thinks they did, remembering a group of people holding down a squirming Peter.

""We'll get to the evacuation later. It's here somewhere, and I bet you've got a story there, too. Back to the book, okay, to finish up."

"What memories I have of the years spent at St. Stephen's primary school. Housed in a plain, orange brick four-storey building with large multi-paned rectangular windows, the seedy slums of Shepherds Bush lay to its right. Off to the left were the humble homes of common Wendell Road with its tough children and the best of all playgrounds!

"Some memories are not so pleasant, such as when I arrived at school drenched from a sudden downpour. I had to undress down to my underwear behind the blackboard that stood high on its tall-as-me three legged easel. I remember shivering with tears of embarrassment as I peeped shyly out of teacher's borrowed cardigan to hear my classmate's titters.

"Another bad memory was when a kindly, military-looking man with a snappy moustache offered me a sweet which was knocked out of my outstretched hand by my irate father. He had been on the Gothic vigil that day. How he berated and blamed me as the man slipped away!

The sadness I felt as I shared with the bereaved family and my stalwart friend, Shirley, on the loss of her twin, the delicate Jackie. We had been an inseparable three. Had we not on our serious discussions after school decided that, yes indeed, babies were born through the bosom. I had my doubts, though. Mother often shared our bath and the poor-lathering wartime soap suds did little to hide her modesty! The other ways of how babies were born, let alone made, as indicated by the crude finger signs and drawings on the park pavement, were just too far-fetched; so too was Auntie Evelyn's statement that it took only one glance from Uncle to get her pregnant again!

"Another dreadful moment at school was then I heard the awful scream of poor Laura as she held her arm aloft. From a thread of skin dangled a huge lump of flesh gouged out by the pointed railing on which she had fallen. Why those iron spikes had not been abolished along with the rest of the precious metal to make munitions, we never knew.

"The line of frightened children snaking its coiled ascent up the cold stone staircase at school to turn the last dreaded corner and finally face the piercing prick of the inoculation needle.

"The kindly gray-haired headmaster whose Irish brogue was so thick and unintelligible that I burst into tears in front of the class when I was unable to relay his simple message.

"The lessons that were so rudely interrupted by the wavering shriek of the air raid siren. Down to the dark, dank basement we would troop. There we'd while away anywhere from five minutes to over an hour plaintively singing 'Somewhere Over the Rainbow' until the continuous one-note All Clear siren sent us streaming out into the bright safety of the day.

"Oh, those bath times, the best of fun ever. As toilet paper was scarce during the war, we used cut up squares of newspaper and old telephone directories hung in readiness on a nail. We'd paste the squares of paper around the bathtub as our picture gallery. The resulting papier mache that went down when the plug was pulled and the subsequent stopped-up drains never concerned me at all!

"The lovely spring Sunday when Peter and I made our First Holy Communion with all our classmates. Peter wore a new short-trousered suit and Mother had made me a white satin dress. A couple of years later on Confirmation Day I was once again stuck with a disliked name, Agnes. The popular choice of Bernadette had been used up by luckier girls.

"The many ball and skipping games we originated in the playground. From the accomplishment of keeping three balls in the air or thrown up against a wall to an accompanying chant; the fast skipping—bumps—inside the beating whip of the stinging rope, as it turned faster and faster to the swiftly sung rhyme. Or the elimination song to decide who was going to be 'it'. Eenie, meenie, mack-ar-ack-ar-rah-rah, Dom-ar-nack-ar-chick-a-chick-a-rah-rah, Om-pom-push.'"

Horst looked at her in amazement. What a memory! "Sounds like a lot of garbled nonsense to me."

"Of course it was," retorted Jill, adding with a sly grin, "That's what German sounded like to me at first! Well, to finish. Almost there, then we'll have a cup of tea before we finish this lot." Horst agreed. He was getting thirsty. Tea would so. Jill read on.

"The games of catch when as the last one left I'd escape the grasp of the grabbing hand at the end of the trailing chain of the 'last roundup' and venture into the boys' sacred territory in my desperation to be victorious.

"Collecting the different shapes of the multi-coloured shrapnel shred off the bombs of the previous night. Peter and I would either swap them at school or add them to our vast collection.

"After school the wonderful times we'd spend in the wilderness of our back garden, avoiding at all costs Father's Victory vegetable garden and his conservatory full of near-ripe tomatoes.

The hateful, hairy spiders waiting in their webs strung across the path, barring my way to the back gate, the quickest exit to Ravenscourt Park down the road. We'd draw spiders in chalk on the path to the outside lavatory where Grandma Field, who hated spiders with a passion, and unable to go to the upstairs toilet, would have to go when visiting. She was an exceptionally large woman unable to see her feet beneath her bulk. That, coupled with failing diabetic eyesight, I doubt she ever noticed our attempts to scare her as she tottered down the path.

"The joy we all felt when Father was reprieved from the call-up. There had been a mix-up in names, so we were told. He continued his nightly Home Guard duty manning an anti-aircraft gun at Wormwood Scrubs, which, ugly and as bad as its name, is also the site of a notorious hard-core prison.

"The screaming pleas from the little lady, Mrs. de Zest, hanging out her window high up in the mansions overlooking our garden, begging us to stop our noisy play. After Mother's tactful talk with this little foreign turbaned lady, we never heard any more complaints. Mother never riled with the neighbours, or indeed with anyone! She never raised her voice or hand in anger, only allowing herself to become 'a little cross' once in a while, silently shown by the tight downward turn of her clamped-together lips!

"We didn't look at all like mother and daughter. How often would I hear, 'You've got none of your mother's pretty hair, brown-eyed looks' from insensitive acquaintances. 'What a pity,' they'd say, adding; 'You must take after your father.' After my many bouts of adolescent petulance, I'd hear, 'Why can't you be more like your dear, sweet mother?' Yet Father did say that although I looked more like his side of the family, I had certain mannerisms and habits of Mother's, none of which he specified. From the clipped tone of his voice and the gleaming glint in his bespectacled eyes, I always took them to be derogatory!"

Jill was silent for a moment as she remembered. A voice from below interrupted her thoughts. "Anyone up there? Jill? Horst?" It was Mother's velvet voice. She appeared on the stairs and said, "I wondered where you'd disappeared to. I've just made a pot of tea," adding on eying the disarray around their feet, "I can see you're busy. Would you like me to bring you each a cup of tea?"

"Yes, please," replied Jill to her mother. "Why don't you come up and join us. We're taking a trip down memory lane and are about to come to your wedding," she added, glancing at the next page of the book.

"No, I'll leave you to reminisce together" replied Mother. "You can show me everything when you come downstairs," then added as she reached the landing, "I may stay and have a quick listen when I come back with the tea. Won't be half a tick."

"While we're waiting for our tea, darling, tell me some more about goings-on with you," suggested Jill. You must have so many stories."

"Let me see," he murmured. "Let me see…" He thought for a moment and then began to speak in a quiet voice.

CHAPTER 9

"Times, in fact, were very pleasant. We still went on our usual Sunday afternoon walks dressed in our best attire. We would leave the house and walk about five miles round trip. Papa and I usually walked ahead with Mama bringing up the rear with my two younger sisters, one in a pushchair. Papa knew every street, bush and tree. He used to point out buildings and tell me interesting anecdotes.

"Our lives passed quietly. One day, however, there was a knock on the door. An air-raid warden asked us all to assemble in the courtyard below. He was going to show the whole family how to put out incendiary bombs in the event one should fall on the roof.

"He showed us how to lift up the heavy bucket full of sand and another with water in which was immersed a small pump. One of us had to pump while the other directed the stream of water towards the fire. We didn't have long to wait to put our expertise into practice.

"That night the sirens sounded for the very first time. We rushed to the cellar and sat listening to heavy gun-fire and the retaliating anti-aircraft guns all around us. We heard bombs falling. As they landed and exploded, the ground beneath us and the entire building shook.

"When the raid was over we rushed upstairs and found that an incendiary bomb had fallen through the roof. We quickly filled up the buckets with water. I pumped and Mama directed the flow towards the burning stick bomb that had landed and fallen on the kitchen table and now lay smouldering on the floor.

"Papa reported our heroic action and Mama was awarded a bronze star for her bravery.

"The air raids became more frequent, so we went to the nearest bunker every night where our family had one of one hundred and fifty available small rooms. Papa was on night work, so it was Mama, my sister, baby sister and me .

""What a great thrill it was when I was allowed to go with Papa to Police Headquarters where one section had been branched off to serve as an Air-raid Command Shelter. There I would sit quietly and watch the teletype-writers clicking away as they reported where and how many bombs had fallen on the city.

"In August 1941 one day there was a particularly heavy raid. I happened to be in the Command Shelter with Papa, the only child privileged to be with the fifty or so chiefs of the various civil defence service—ambulance, anti-looting, fire, anti-aircraft—who were answering telephones and rushing around with pieces of paper and giving directions to the many uniformed women.

"The ground shook and the walls shuddered. Everyone looked very anxious although the shelter was supposed to be completely bomb proof. Anxiety turned to fear when the bombs rained down nonstop about a mile away. The time between the exploding bombs became less as the raid came closer. We all thought, 'This is it. We've had it.'

"This was the first of the carpet bombings, the Americans by day and the English by night. Ten fast fighters would drop flares to illuminate one section of the city, followed by a thousand bombers that would drop their deathly cargo on the pin-pointed area, hoping either to destroy the factories, the river and the bridges, or, when it became out and out total war, anything that lay below.

"Several hours of heavy barrage went by. When we were at last able to leave the bunker after the all-clear siren, a whole new world lay before us.

"Eighty-five percent of the city had been destroyed. Between the crumbling, burning buildings and flattened rubble, we heard the cries of the injured and wails for the dead. Frightened and tense survivors sought out family members. New vistas had sprung up and we could see from one end of the city to the other. Papa silently blessed the bunkers that had protected his wife and children.

"One of Papa's duties was to set out and search for any planes that had been shot down—friend or foe. Very few German fighters, as compared to the thousands of enemy planes in the skies, were involved, counter attack being mainly from the ground with searchlights and anti-aircraft guns. During this one raid there were about one hundred and seventy English Royal Air Force bombers shot down.

"Papa told me that when he arrived at the scene the injured crewmen were being transported to the nearest hospital. The dead were left until last when they would be taken away for burial. The names, ranks and numbers of all downed bomber crews were recorded and passed on to the Red Cross who would notify next-of-kin in England, America and Germany.

"I remember he brought home a bar of English chocolate which he had retrieved from one of the crashed bombers!"

"Hmm," said Jill softly, thinking it better to keep a respectful silence for a moment. It all seemed so far behind them. Yet they were both still part of those grim days. It was their childhood.

"On a more cheerful note, dear Horst," she said lightheartedly. "I will continue according to the book." She had heard Mother on her way up with a tray of tea and called out, "Just in time, I'm going to tell Horst about 'doing our bit'."

Between the leaves of the book lay a tattered programme with two black and white pictures on its cover. The top photo showed a large troupe of tiny, blurry-faced young girls wearing white bows, sparkly costumes and silver tap shoes. The taller ones are standing in the back row with hands held provocatively on hip. The medium sized girls in the middle row are kneeling on one knee with both hands pertly placed atop a kneecap. The babies sit demurely cross-legged on the floor. Above the ensemble strung in a downward arc in front of a black curtain are a bevy of silver stars each with a capital letter spelling out the word MERLWYN.

"Doing your bit?" Horst looked puzzled.

"Yes, just like you. Listen both of you." Mother put down the tray.

"World War II raged six long years in Europe from 1939 to 1945, during which time every Englishman, woman and child did 'his bit', or share, for the war effort.

"I did my bit for the cause of peace by entertaining the poor wounded soldiers returning from the battlefields of Europe. One of a large troupe of girls ranging in age from three to fourteen, at age seven, I was one of the youngest, thinnest, plainest and least talented. of Gonda Merlwyn's Famous Wonder Children.

"My mother enrolled me in this dance school at its inception when classes were held in Gonda's living room. I became one of her star pupils, not because of my ability to tap, go up on my toes, sing, do acrobatics, or be beautifully cute. My seniority status and endurance along with that of my mother's to unfailingly pay for the lessons, earned me my star status. We'd also stuck with the troupe during the thick and thin of a growing show biz.

"Those endless classes where patient mothers, doing their bit by knitting-for-the-troops bountiful balaclavas, warm socks and mittens, sat silently clicking and proudly watching. After day school, private voice lessons attempted to help me hit the high note for my solo song, 'In my sweet little Alice Blue Gown', but all to no avail. Finally a low C was substituted for the top one I failed to reach! I was eternally grateful that the pianist played loudly enough to drown out my pitiful attempt. My voice was further diminished from reaching the audience by the loud laughter of my siblings in the 'gods' above, the chatting parents and relatives in the stalls, all to the accompaniment of the raucous whistles of the servicemen in the front rows in the blackness somewhere beyond the stage.

"However, as soon as the spotlight dazzled me and the piano gave me its cue, I shrieked out those songs; "Johnny's Got a Zero" with appropriate flying motions of my arms, "Easter Parade" with frilled parasol, and my best number, Oh, You Beautiful Doll" when the audience, needing little encouragement, roared out the final refrain of "Oh, oh, oh, oh, OH, you beautiful Doll." I ended up with a short snappy tap dance that was easier and more enjoyable than the song for both me and the audience.

"During our long journey by bus and train in the gloomy days of wartime London, dark without its bright street lamps, many a time, on hearing the wailing siren and seeing searchlight beams scanning the night sky for German bombers, Mother and I were forced to duck into an air raid shelter to await the All Clear. We always arrived out of breath just before curtain time.

"Backstage was crazy! We all came with our mothers, many of whom had helped make the fantastic array of costumes, goodness only knows how, in those days of clothes rationing. There were about forty items on the program counting both solo and chorus turns. There in the Green Room, which was usually a narrow backstage passage, Gonda's girls gathered with one solitary boy. In most numbers, this simple, smiling, simpering youth of eight or nine played the role of the boy hero or male fantasy figure.

"Our mothers applied our make up, and arranged our freshly ironed costumes ready to be grabbed and donned easily between acts. My hair was freshly curled, a la Shirley Temple, after a sleepless night lying on corkscrew-shaped rags and rolled newspaper curlers.

"The show's final number was always a patriotic one where the entire ensemble from babes to teens, attired in red, white and blue costumes, sang and danced their hearts out as the piano belted, the audience cheered, whistled and waved Union Jack flags. The grand finale arrived in the shapely form of one of the teens, who danced down the stage steps to the front row, where she daintily slid on the lap of one of the `poor wounded soldiers', who blushed with embarrassment, yet pleased to be chosen, as she sang, caressed and saluted him.

"I performed in many town hall shows all over London, and sometimes in local parks on a hastily improvised stage. In one such show, I tripped going on stage, and Gonda gave me a vicious push. Although hurt, what a trouper I was, as I continued dancing, singing and smiling, in spite of blood and pain running down my leg. Mother was furious! This incident was the straw that broke my long history with the Merlwyn Babes, along with the consistent grumbling of my father. He had lost all patience with the long, laborious nightly efforts spent curling my dead-straight hair. Coupled with my mother's neglect of him and home, along with Gonda's insistence that I take and pay for extra tuition in order to keep my star status, that was the end of it all.

"I think my mother was tired, too! We'd done our bit for the war effort!"

Jill closed the book. Mother looked pensive. Horst laughed uproariously. "Which one is you?" he asked. Jill pointed to an indistinguishable blur kneeling in the second row.

"And those are Auntie Bibbie's young daughters," she explained, pointing to the bottom row of blurry cross-legged tots.

"I'll take your word for it, Jill. I'd never have recognized any of you if you hadn't told me."

CHAPTER 10

"This must be the photo you mentioned to Mother, Jill," said Horst passing it to his mother-in-law. "It's your wedding. Why, you've changed hardly at all," said Horst, ever the charmer. "I'd have no trouble recognizing you."

"Oooh, you are kind, Horse," she replied, glancing at the faces in the photo. Jill smiled at her mother's attempt to get her tongue around the 't.'

"Stay a while longer, Mother," pleaded Jill, "and help me out with the people at your wedding. Squeeze up next to me here," she said pointing to the top stair. I'm going to read from my book."

"Just for a little while. Can't stay long. Your father's waiting for his tea, too." She and her son-in-law scrutinized the photo as Jill began.

"The official wedding photo was taken on their wedding day outside the stone parish church in Hammersmith. Seated in the center is Ivy Alexandra Field wearing a halo of pearls atop a veil covering her bobbed blond wavy hair. Seated next to his bride is Reginald James Guy Martin with a receding hairline. Standing behind them is the bridal party of nine.

Jill paused. "On the back of the picture it says in your handwriting, Mother, 'To Mamma and Dadda from Ivie and Reg—September 6th 1931'. That's what you called your parents, isn't it?" Mother nodded. Jill was dubious about the double consonants, but then her mother had never been the best of spellers. "And did you spell your name with an 'ie' to match up with you sisters, Evie, Bibbie and Lollie?"

"Absolutely not," Mother replied indignantly. Jill decided not to argue. Her mother had tried many versions of her name, the most recent being Ivory.

That was when Evie, with whom sister Ivy had the love-hate relationship of close siblings, declared on becoming a first-time grandmother, that never would she answer to Grandma, Granny, Nana or Nan, choosing instead, 'Mamie after the best-selling book, play and film 'Auntie Mame'.

Jill continued. "Ivy and Reg were both approaching their twenty-fifth birthdays, she in October and he in December."

Mother laughed. "Why on earth did you put that in? Telling all my secrets!" (It was a no-no to mention that she was six weeks older than her husband.)

"He, 5'10 and she 5'7" were considered tall in those days…" 'Well, Mother, that's what you were always telling Peter and me as we were shooting up to 6'6" and 5'11" as you shrank down.' It was Jill's turn to laugh. "I know I didn't reach 6' because at one time I actually had to stretch an inch to qualify as a six footer. Remember, Horst, I told that's what I had to do to join the San Francisco Tall Club. And," she added, turning to her mother, "don't deny that at your tennis club you made a beeline for Father because he was the tallest boy there."

"Don't give ALL my secrets away, Jill dear" admonished her mother. "Finish your tea and get on with the photo. I can't stay here much longer."

Jill gulped down her tea and continued reading. "I've always thought how Father, a shy, introverted youth, second to the youngest in a family of nine and deprived of a loving father and his mother's attention, had the good fortune to come into contact with Mother's family of extroverts. They drew him into the activities of the social and tennis club at their parish church where Father was an altar boy. Both fifteen years old at the time, they became beaux and nine years later united in this ceremony. In 1981 they celebrated their Golden Wedding, 50 years."

"I remember that, Mother," declared Horst. "It was quite a reunion of all the family. All Jill's aunts, uncles, cousins, brothers and wives and all your grandchildren, Mother. I hadn't been part of such a huge family celebration since our own wedding, you know, and that was quite overwhelming, too!"

Jill continued, "Standing directly behind them are tall Grandpa Field and short Grandma, both large and imposing figures. Grandma Martin is lean, narrow shouldered, long of neck, as I am, and dignified, as I am not! She is wearing an elegant, big-brimmed black cloche hat that makes her as tall as 6' Grandpa.

"To the right are two bridesmaids holding bouquets of carnations with feathery ferns. They are dressed in shiny satin, ankle-length flounced dresses with Juliet caps atop their heads. Bibby is the only dark-haired sister. Madeleine,

Father's baby sister, looks like Auntie Edie, the unmarried sister who lived with Grandma Martin.

"Auntie Madie, with her pleasant pipe-smoking husband and three daughters remained on the fringe of all our family activities. Although they lived close by, she preferred her husband's genteel family connections and the social life of my cousins' private convent school. We kept our respected distances—for, granted, Madie's brother's in-laws could be rather overpowering, both in size and personality. I visited the family on a few occasions, usually birthdays, but my brothers, maybe because they were noisy boys, very seldom, if ever!

"Well, Mother, I have remembered correctly, haven't I?" She glanced anxiously at her mother. "There wasn't much love lost between you and your sister-in-law, was there?" Mother harrumphed and said, "Get on with it, Jill."

"Frank, an older brother of Father's whom we scarcely knew, was married to one of the chorus girls in the famous Tiller troupe. He also had traveled extensively in South America, which is why he supposedly named his only child, Juanita—a cousin I regret never meeting."

"Well, my dear daughter," interjected Mother. "Who's fault was that?"

"I know, all mine, Mother," confessed Jill. "Let me tell you, Horst, that I once had the opportunity of meeting this long lost cousin. It was about ten years ago when Juanita turned up out of the blue after her father's death at Auntie Madie's who, in turn, promptly walked her down to chat over a cup of tea with Mother. At the time I was dirty and disheveled up a ladder spring cleaning, and by the time I did respond to Mother's phone call to come and meet this cousin, it was too late. She had already left."

"Of Father's other five sisters, two had died of tuberculosis at ages seven and thirty-four, leaving three (who are not in the picture as they were not bridesmaids). They are Auntie Edie, Grandma Martin's companion and Auntie May, married, with the apt name of Mrs. Lean, childless and lead soprano in the church choir. This aunt played a huge role in the life of Mother's sister Evie who had lived long with Uncle Sydney and their five children. It was this Auntie May when working as a clerk in a Chiswick funeral home who recognized the name of a deceased male brought in one day. It was Evelyn's first husband. May quickly passed the word on to Mother and Father who informed Evelyn and Sydney. Next day they got married and legitimized their union."

"Nothing's sacred," sighed Mother. "How many more confidences are you going to expose, Jill?"

"It's all family history," retorted Jill, ready for the next paragraph, fortunately not another expose. "Last is little Auntie Bobbie (Mary Frances whose nickname referred to her bobbed hair), a petite woman with the small Martin head, and with Grandma Martin's soft tremulous voice and tinkling laughter. This auntie with her stocky curly-headed Welsh husband and two children later moved into and lived for many, many years in the little house on the corner with the Gothic window.

"It was in that room where I lay snugly in my bed beneath the window with the wartime blackout curtain open to the dark outside. No street lamps were allowed during the nightly blitz. As I peeped from under my warm blanket, I could see out of the corner of my eye the wooden cut-out life-size figures of two characters from Alice in Wonderland. The Walrus and the Carpenter appeared grotesque as arm-in-arm they loomed menacingly in the gloom of the room. By daylight it was obvious that these two humorous and delightful characters, one with pointed tusks and bristling whiskers and the other with dwarfish features topped by a red square hat, were innocuous and friendly. But in the shadows of the night-time room, enlivened by a ghostly moon shining through the awesome Gothic window, they appeared alarming as they threatened to grab me. I dared not breath, let alone move an inch in bed, as I became frozen with fright.

"Goodness gracious, Jill. I never knew you felt like that," cried Mother, aghast. "Your father and I would have taken them away, had we known." Jill assured her that it was just childhood fantasy and no harm was done. "No more shocks, please," pleaded Mother.

"The bridesmaids on the left of the picture are Auntie Lollie, Stoney, Mother's office friend, and Auntie Evie, almost Mother's double, except for her thick tight curls, cheeky expression and defiant chin. She was a year younger than Mother with a birthday falling three days earlier. Since the sisters always received identical presents from their parents, Mother never ever had a surprise package to open!

"You hadn't forgotten that, had you, Mother?" Without waiting for an answer, Jill added, pointing to the photo. "Final page coming up."

"I missed out the thickset short young man with a white parting dividing his dark slicked-down hair, Evie's first husband, who faded from the picture shortly after this wedding. A short-lived marriage of incompatibility, Auntie Evie soon left him." Mother's urgent voice interrupted.

"Let me see that, Jill. You've got it all wrong," she said, pointing to the man. "That's your Father's best man, Charlie Piff. They were best friends from school and church. That is certainly not Evelyn's husband, although she was married at the time."

"Thank goodness you're here to correct it, Mother," said Jill, apologetically. "Glad you put the record straight. I do remember you telling me how you helped Auntie Evie move her possessions out of their flat. As her husband came in the front door, you and Evie left out the back window!"

"Psst," whispered Horst. "Ask Mother about the twins or triplets in Father's family. Do you know anything, Mother?"

"Yes, let me see," She struggled to remember. "Yes, Jill. Your Grandma Martin was one of eleven children, three of whom were triplets—two boys and a girl. Your great grandmother breast fed the weakest baby, the girl. The boys were bottle fed. Only the girl survived."

Jill realized she'd mixed up which baby got the bottle and which the breast. "Thanks, Mother. Nothing like getting the facts straight for posterity." She then reiterated the final sentence of the book. "After a short-lived marriage of incompatibility, Auntie Evie left her first husband. Out of the frying pan into the fire she went, straight into the open arms of Uncle Sydney, a stern, balding, older solicitor who was handling her divorce. He swept her off her feet to his practice in the country where he sired five children." Mother nodded.

"It was to their home in Stony Stratford, about sixty miles north of London, that we three, Peter, Junior and I, were evacuated during the worst part of the London blitz. All parents were encouraged to send their children into the safety of the countryside and made to feel guilty if they didn't!

""I remember being there for years and years. However, I learned much later from Mother that it was only for a very long six weeks, at the end of which Father came down one weekend to take one of us back home to London."

Jill relaxed with a sigh of relief after her bout of reading. Mother collected the teacups and went downstairs to tend to her husband. Besides, she'd had enough memories for one day. "I'll catch up with your book some other time," she called from the landing below.

CHAPTER 11

Jill and Horst spread out on the top stair. "Come on, Horst. Surely all that prompts you to tell a story," she said, rummaging around in some of the loose photos. "There's even some of your old family pictures here," she added, handing him one. Horst had his story ready to go.

"In Germany we had been living in Ludwigshafen on Rhein for a long time. Mama was beginning to miss her family, especially her mother, and her home-town of Berlin. Opa Schaar, her father, had died of consumption in his early fifties—or so it is said. Rumours abounded, though, that his premature death was more likely from over-indulgence of wine and women! The pub had been sold and Oma moved in with her son, Mama's brother, the favourite child.

"Mama would telephone and write repeatedly to Oma, pleading with her to come for an extended visit. But Oma always refused on the basis that she was needed in Berlin with her son, who any day would be called up into the army. As for my father, from all appearances it looked as if he would not be enlisted and would remain in his police officer's position in Ludwigshafen.

"On Oma's very rare visits she would make the long train journey and stay as short a time as possible. Her stay with us was a joy to all. She would cook, clean, listen patiently to her daughter and cuddle and spoil her grandchildren endlessly. Whenever she felt that she was in the way or that the family wanted their privacy, she would retire to her room and spend hours alone, peacefully knitting.

"When she returned home after her last visit to us, her son was drafted into the army. His wife, my aunt, a fat jolly woman and her two children were later evacuated to a farm in Bavaria in Southern Germany. Oma went with them and from then on, all Mama's pleas went unheeded.

"Mama made me send one desperate telegram saying, 'Everybody sick. Desperately in need of help. Please come immediately'. It went unanswered. Mama could never understand why her mother preferred staying with her brother's family whom, we all knew, treated her as a servant, was derided by her daughter-in-law and name-called by her grandchildren!"

"Strange, isn't it, Horst," murmured Jill, "how both grandmothers favoured their sons?"

"Well, you're a chip off the old block yourself, Jill," he teased. It took her a moment to understand what he meant. Of course, what else could she do but favour her three sons. She had no daughters! Continuing, Horst wound up his story.

"1942 and Papa, a great worrier and a pessimist by nature, had finally gone into hospital. Over the following eighteen months he spent several two week sessions being treated for and recovering from a stomach ulcer. He required a special diet along with rest, relief and respite from his heavy responsibilities. His absences from the police force were facilitated by delegating his duties to two very capable under-assistants, whom Papa once admitted, were as capable as he, if not more so, at doing the job.

"He suffered enormously from the pain of the ulcer. When he first went into hospital, even the weight of the sheet on his stomach was too much to bear.

"Mama was given yet another award, for Motherhood. She received the Bronze Medal, the auspicious Mutter Kreuz, signifying that she had produced four German children to the glory of the Fatherland.

"In fact Mama and Papa had five children in all. The oldest was me, followed by my two sisters and my younger brother who was born at the end of our evacuation to the country. In between the two girls Mama gave birth to another daughter who was born with an open spine, spina bifida. The baby mercifully died a natural death after three days, or so Mama was led to believe. It was the era of Hitler's annihilation of imperfect beings and the baby would undoubtedly not have been allowed to live. It was only after the war that she learned the baby had been given a lethal injection." Jill shuddered, gasping audibly.

"My second sister who was born the following year bears a large birthmark in the exact spot of the opening in the dead baby's spine."

"Goodness gracious me!" remarked Jill weakly, recovering from the shock. "Does she know about her older sister?"

""I'm sure she does," replied Horst. "Next time we see her, remind me to ask her for an unveiling."

"I hope she's not shy," retorted Jill as she turned the page to a story about her Grandma Field, her mother's mother. "Want to take a break, Horst, after that awful revelation" she asked. "I've got a parallel grandma story here in the book." He nodded and Jill began to read.

"In England at this time we had moved from the little house on the corner with the green front door and Gothic window. Mother and Father had managed to mortgage their first home, a semi-detached house, a mile away in Chiswick. These mirror-image three-storey boxes resembled row after row of Siamese twins joined at the seam." She paused and glanced at Horst for his reaction to her clever simile.

"When I first arrived in England," he said with a smile, "I'd never seen such houses before—all alike, and I was always getting lost. I wondered how anyone could find their own home."

Jill thought this ridiculous. If anything, she'd had the same problem with the huge blocks of apartment buildings in Germany. "Just listen, Horst," she urged.

"The houses were identical in every aspect save for the occupant's personal expression, such as the colour of the well or poorly maintained exterior, window dressings and well-kept or unkempt front garden. That gave them individuality." It was Horst's turn to harrumph.

"The low brick wall in the front was topped by a thick evergreen privet hedge that kept Father busy with his shears while one of us children swept up the clippings. A side entrance led down to a large back garden with flower borders on either side surrounding a central lawn that Father criss-crossed with crazy paving.

"A shaky swing supported by a rickety wooden frame was lodged between the neighbouring fence and the brick wall of the scullery. I would spend many a pensive hour or petulant mood slowly and silently swinging gently to and fro or twist the tope tightly to unravel in a dizzying spin. Sometimes with a push from Peter, I'd swing up the top of the pear tree that overlooked an exclusive private tennis club. In later years, whenever I could induce Peter to leave his teenage friends playing billiards in his attic bedroom, and the courts were empty, he and I would nip over the fence and sneak in a game of tennis."

"Okay," said Jill. "That lays the background to Grandma Field who every six months moved between Mother and Auntie Bibbie who both had ground-floor rooms. Grandma couldn't climb up stairs with her sore leg. Her two daughters were both caring and compassionate of the not so old lady who was in her early sixties.

"The day of her move was a major undertaking. Every member of the two families scurried back and forth carrying Grandma's belongings, climaxing when Father and Uncle Jack escorted and supported her to her new nest for the next half year.

"When Grandma came to live with us there were drastic changes for the whole family. Our standard of living certainly improved tremendously as we shared in her generosity and affluence. We children had to be more conscious of noisy play and tip-toe outside her room, which was our former dining-room with the French windows leading to the beloved swing.

"One of my daily chores was to read the Radio Times to Grandma who was blind. As I read she would absorb and memorize the programmes and plan her radio listening, her other life-line besides her busy telephone. As I slowly read and re-read all the items so she could assimilate the information, I would catch her removing her dark glasses to wipe the tears from the dead white pupils of her unseeing eyes. Upon leaving her clinicy-smelling room of acrid insulin injections and fading body function odours mingled with antiseptics, fragrant talc and eau-de-cologne, I would feel humbled by this unfortunate old lady. With her short severely combed-back gray hair, once strawberry blond and long, she sat regal and proud in her voluminous black dress with the white dots. A strand of bulbous pearls encircled her short neck with minute pearl earrings in her tiny pink lobes. However pleased to return to the cozy family room, I was proud of my special assignment.

"Mother's chores were more than doubled, yet she coped uncomplainingly with her young children and hard-working demanding husband. Father, who expected his daily meat and two veg meal to be served up on the dot, spent his days in his sanitary engineering office, a job apparently vital to the war effort for he was call-up exempt. Most evenings he spent on duty at his home-guard unit where he proudly wore a khaki uniform, the brass buttons of which I spat and polished while Peter spat and shined the heavy army boots.

"Grandma was ultra demanding and entirely dependent on her daughter for her specially-prepared dietary meals and occasional lapses in her desire for rich foods. "Here's a treat for you," Mother would sometimes whisper as she handed us hot toast dripping with Grandma's precious black-market butter, an unknown luxury in post-war England.

Jill paused. "Mother was a first class nurse, you know, Horst. She had always wanted to be a nurse but Grandma considered it not a good enough occupation for her oldest daughter. Ironic, isn't it." She turned back to the book.

"Grandma's diabetic illness dictated daily injections. The blood and pus bandage covering her never-to-heal ulcerative leg also required a daily change, as did disposal of the contents of her commode. That's when Mother would utter a quiet call, not wishing to upset Grandma's pride by reminding her that she too was mortal like the rest of us. Then with pinched nostrils she would sweep through the kitchen with the offensive contents of the covered pan held at arms length from her body as we quickly opened doors and cleared a pathway to the outside lavatory.

"Another of Mother's tasks which although tiring and time-consuming, I think she relished, was the buying and preparation of Grandma's generous Christmas gifts to all her grandchildren. Each child received a huge carton filled by Mother with toys, books and goodies.

"Mother comforted and cared for the proud matriarch whose massive size increased as her spirit waned, ever despising her own increasing helplessness. Mother was a true Florence Nightingale. In a way, Grandma in her own fight against diabetes and her despair at losing control of her life was a victim of a war against illness, old age and loss of independence.

"Yet, with her sightless eyes, painful leg and little recognition of her caring daughters, she never lost her unswerving courage and unfailing belief in her sons. Grandma was constantly on the phone to the remaining son, reassuring and being reassured that all was going well with the shops, as he mismanaged her affairs and drank himself to death!

"It's really strange, a quirk of Fate, how the three brothers who were Grandma Field's pride and joy, all died early, leaving the four sisters to inherit the fruits of Grandpa's labour.

"Charlie, the favourite son, the second son after four daughters, died of cirrhosis of the liver, leaving practically nothing to his estranged wife and small daughter. Buxom Dorothy, as the story goes, a peroxide blond barmaid married Charlie for his money. I understand she never really became a part of the Field family, although she bore the name." Jill paused and looked up from the book. "I wonder whatever became of them?"

Horst laughed. "Don't ask me. If you don't know, I certainly don't!'

"Of course, now I remember," continued Jill quickly. She married the chauffeur of the hired car service Grandma used from time to time. And that wasn't long after Uncle's funeral! Last paragraph coming up, Horst, then we'll return to you."

"How their child, Christine, a pretty girl with flaxen hair like her mother, had everything that we four didn't. We really felt like the poor country cousins at her birthday parties and on our official Christmas Day visits. She had beautiful expensive clothes—and I was wearing Peter's cast-off school raincoat; a birthday table groaning with all kinds of delicious goodies while we were still heavily rationed! Such an expensive array of toys were hers—and we had to make do with the empty wooden crates in Grandma Field's shopyard. Covering Auntie and Uncle's bed was the most beautiful plump, silky rose eiderdown, the likes of which I had only ever seen in black and white at the cinema. All we had were gray Utility blankets. Nothing like that, for sure!

"This poor little rich girl, I faintly recall," added Jill, "grew up endlessly seeking information about her father, Charlie, who had died when she was very young. Her mother, Dorothy, refused to tell her anything. My own mother swore that the truth about her brother would never come from her or any of us. Better that Christine, in her ignorance, think only the best of her father. Mother was not vindictive."

CHAPTER 12

"Phew!" Jill turned the page and saw that the long story of her wartime evacuation had come up. "Time for a breather, Horst. The long awaited saga of the evacuation is next."

But he wanted to continue. "I've got a great story, too."

"Well, you go ahead, lieb, before you forget what you want to say. All I have to do is to read mine from the book." She earmarked her page with the little Union Jack flag and turned her attention to her husband.

"In Ludwigshafen there really was not too much fuss or commotion going on within our family. If there was, I certainly wasn't aware of it. But by then war was almost an every day occurrence to us all.

"However, it was decided that we would be evacuated to the country to a small village of one hundred people about fifty miles from Ludwigshafen. Our apartment had suffered some damage during the raid, although Mama and my two sisters had been safe in the bunker.

"Papa arranged transportation for us and we loaded up a few necessary possessions into the truck and set off for Erfenstein, our evacuation village. We would be there for four years, at the end of which time my younger brother was born.

"When we arrived in the village the long-established inhabitants were unwelcoming as they had previously been forced to requisition part of their homes to evacuees such as us. I noticed that many of the villagers had a strange look about them—simple appearing, in fact. Mama explained that this was due to years of inter-marriage between the families over the preceding generations.

"Papa had originally wanted us to go to Uncle Spielhagen's estate in East Prussia, the place I had visited years ago for the stag hunt. However, being in the eastern part of Germany and close to the Polish border, it would have been a far more dangerous place to be sent. Our lives would certainly have been much harder and we may not have survived the onslaught of the advancing Russian troops. This proves to me how implicitly Papa believed that the Russians would never be able to advance into, or even come close, to German territory. Yet, after liberating Poland from German rule, they marched right through and into Germany. Our Aunt Clara Spielhagen later told us how they ordered every female from teenage up to lie down in the street to be raped! Whether or not she was a victim is unknown for sure, although I remember her voice was strained at the telling.

"Papa quite sincerely believed that the day would come when the secret weapon promised by Hitler would make Germany victorious. When that glorious day arrived he would tell me that he would be rewarded with a large estate in the Ukraine. We would have lots of servants. The inferior persons, the Untermenchen, would work for us and we would be their masters. Papa was not a sadistic person who relished ruling over slaves. A civil servant all his life, I think he enjoyed the hypothetical thought of being master of his own estate, savouring the anticipation of such an eventuality purely as an escapist dream.

"We were assigned half a small house, the other half occupied by the owners. To reach our portion we had to intrude on their property and continually apologized for passing through their living room. None of us liked this arrangement.

"We had no gas; electricity was for lighting purposes only and not to be used for cooking. So we cooked over a large fireplace in which we burned logs to cook, boil water and heat the room. Wood was collected from the forest close by, chopped up as kindling and stored in the back yard with the chickens.

"It was my chore to chop the wood. The pesky chickens fluttered around foraging and pecking for food. One day they distracted my attention. The hefty blow of the axe missed the log and chopped off my left thumb instead. One alert chicken rushed in, grabbed the thumb and ran off with it!

"Mama, Mama," I hollered. "The chicken's run off with my thumb." As she couldn't make head or tail of my garbled cries, I ran into the house and help up my bleeding stump. All she could do for the moment was to wrap it in a towel to stop the bleeding.

"Strangely enough I felt no pain whatsoever until that night when it throbbed and throbbed and began to swell. Unfortunately there was no hospital close enough to walk to, so I had to wait until the following day for transport to come and take me to the nearest town fifty miles away. The hospital was full of wounded soldiers who were given preferential treatment. However, the doctor gave me a total anesthetic and did a perfunctory job of sewing up the overlapping skin over the raw stump—and when I came to, I remember asking him if I could still be a soldier when I grew up. I must have been delusional for that's the last thing I wanted to be. Unfortunately dirt had entered the wound and it became infected, giving me weeks and weeks of trouble and pain until it healed.

"A few days prior to the accident Papa had somehow arranged to get me a bicycle. How pleased I'd been for I had long yearned for one. It was the type with its only brake on the left-hand handle. With my left hand heavily bandaged, painful and immobilized, I was unable to ride it properly. I persevered until I finally fell off onto my sore hand and couldn't ride anymore. This was, indeed, a great tragedy in my young life.

"Time wore on. By 1942/43 we felt the ground shake almost every night and saw in the distance the destruction of the far-away big cities. The sky was constantly aglow with the burning buildings and bombed chemical factories of our city.

"Papa's visits became infrequent. During 1943 he managed a brief visit every month. How grateful he felt even for that. Mama, I think, suffered somewhat from being away from her home and from the brush-off treatment of the locals. She also missed being mistress of her spacious, pleasant apartment and the privacy of her own home.

"On one of Papa's visits we knew he had something to tell us because of the smug smile on his face. Yet, in his usual non-commital, secretive manner, he kept silent, all the while hinting that he had some good news. He changed out of his uniform as usual, paced up and down, smiling and throwing out hints, yet telling us nothing. After the first few hours of careful probing and receiving only Papa's self-satisfied smile, Mama's even temper erupted for he was enjoying her frustration! She said disgustedly, "'What do I care! Keep your silly secret to yourself.' He thereupon quickly pointed to his shoulder, indicating that he had been promoted. He then proudly brought out the certificate personally signed by Hitler.

"By 1944 food became very scarce. Papa arranged with some farmers who had been drafted into the police force to give us food in exchange for days off. The problem was how to get to the villages where the farmers had their farms with their stock of food. Mama could not leave my youngest sister who was only two years old or take her with her. Besides Mama was pregnant with my brother. So I elected to go.

"Off I went on the trusty old bicycle with a big rucksack on my back. A tall thin blue-eyed, brown-haired eleven year old youth, I pedaled away the whole day, often to arrive in the dark, stay overnight with the farmer, collect the food and cycle back home.

"By that time the enemy had started strafing the valley with their hunter fighter planes. Anything that moved was shot at. This meant that as I cycled along the road, I had to be alert and keep my eyes and ears open.

"As soon as the planes were heard humming in the distance, I'd drop the bike and run and hide in the woods. I found it a very exciting game and didn't mind the danger at all.

"We had a three mile walk to and from school through the woods. Often our group of boys would deliberately stand in the open, wait for the planes to approach, then gesticulate and make rude signs to the pilots—waiting until the last moment before the guns on the cockpit started their rat-a-tat-tat to make a spurt to the shelter of the forest, a nearby cave or a handy rock. It was so thrilling! Sadly though, we did lose one boy to a sniper's bullet.

"Erfenstein 1943," mused Horst. "We'd been there over a year and I'd rejoined the junior Hitler Youth. One of the tallest, cleverest and brightest of the village boys was fifteen year old Fritz. He was the leader of the local group. Although he had invited me to join, I didn't have much choice anyway, for it was expected that every youth join such an organization.

"We would meet once or twice a week in an old wooden hut in the valley between two hills, each with an old ruined castle on top. That is when I first heard the story about Erfenstein and Spengenburg, the names of the two old castles.

"Two robber baron brothers lived in either of the castles. One was unmarried and the other had a beautiful wife. It was decided to build a leather bridge between the two castles to facilitate their visits to each other, rather than going the long way down through the valley. Unbeknownst to the one brother, his golden-haired wife and bachelor brother had fallen in love and the bridge was used for their trysts. When the brother discovered the treachery, he waited until his brother was midway on the bridge and took his revenge by cutting it down, plunging his brother to his death.

"The local junior Hitler Youth which I belonged to was, as I've said before, really a glorified Boy Scout troop. We had to attend regularly, achieve merit badges and wear a uniform. The Hitler Youth organization presented Fritz, as leader, with the full smart attire of starched brown shirt, corduroy shorts and leather belt. How I bullied poor Mama to get me such a uniform. Clothing was scarce and unobtainable and for once I didn't get my own way. Fritz told me to cheer up and join in the patriotic sing-song and he allowed me to hold his Hitler Youth dagger.

"The highest honour of all was to be awarded a Hitler Youth dagger that was worn in a sheath on the leather belt. Punctuality, good attendance, merit badges and good sportsmanship were the requisites. Although I passed all these tests, I still didn't get the coveted dagger. Very few were available as the scarce material was needed for munitions. As each week went by, I hoped to receive the long-promised award, but it was not to be. I had suffered through the good sportsman's test for nothing! This was a fool's test. The seniors would create a noise by beating the bushes in the forests. I then had to hold open a large bag to catch the imaginary birds—die Elvedritsche—as they flew out!

"I did receive a dagger from Papa, a special one with a deer's hoof as its hilt. But I lost it! I told my best friend, Werner, that I'd searched everywhere and couldn't find it. He told me he knew someone who was a psychic and could tell me where the dagger was. I didn't go and I never found the dagger.

"One sinister side of the Hitler Youth was the pseudo guarding of the Russian prisoners, the men and women forced labour. We were told to report any attempted escape or any of them seen on the run. I never had the chance to obtain that badge either.

"Erfenstein, being located in a forest area, had a small paper mill. Werner, the son of the owner, and I spent a lot of time picking apples in his father's orchard. Anyhow, in the factory, wood, along with old rags collected from miles around, were made into clothing material.

"In 1943/44 Russian women prisoners were employed as forced labour to make these clothes. They lived and slept in purpose-built caves in the hillside. It was rumoured—and I never talked to Werner about this—that his father, the owner was a sadistic old man who several times a week took some of the prisoners to the caves where they were beaten up. It was further whispered around that he had many mistresses among the Russian women. Fritz, too, would boast of his conquests with the Russian girls. I found this exciting, yet was never invited on one of these adventurous trips." Jill burst out laughing.

"Well, I know I was only eleven years old," admitted Horst. "But, Jill, listen to this. At the end of the war the owner was found mutilated and dead in his factory.

"One day a high-up Nazi officer came to the village. Fritz collected the whole Hitler Youth band for this occasion. The officer told us that every village must prepare for bombing raids and be ready in the unlikely event that the enemy would arrive. We were to dig a tunnel into a hill to be used as an air-raid shelter. The work was to be carried out on Sundays as everyone was busy during the week. Inexpensive timber was collected to form the supports of the tunnel.

"We started digging one Sunday and after about ten weekends had progressed about thirty yards into the hill. But our inexperienced bracing was too weak to hold up the tunnel. It collapsed, killing one of the village boys who was buried alive under the falling scaffolding.

"One Sunday a short wyhile after this incident, I was at Fritz's house. An old Catholic priest in a shabby, stained cassock was holding a service in the front room. This was a dangerous thing to do, for although religion was tolerated during Hitler's regime, it definitely was not encouraged. Priests of any sect were supposed to be war sympathizers. The Protestant priests in Germany, being state-employed, were enlisted into active service as officers, not necessarily to fight at the Front, but mostly to spread the word of the Party. However, ever since Hitler had been awarded the Christ Medal by the Pope, the highest honour to be bestowed by the Catholic Church, Hitler had turned a blind eye to Catholic religious practices.

"The priest could have been in serious trouble with the Nazi authorities, had he been reported. During his sermon he explained away the tunnels' failure and the boy's death as punishment for working on God's day of rest. He then proceeded to denounce the Nazis for ordering the work to be carried out on a Sunday at all." Horst's voice trailed off. Jill noticed his face somewhat strained, or maybe it was the shadows across his features as they sat there in the oncoming twilight.

She reached for and held on to his hand. "How light-hearted my evacuation was compared to yours, Horst."

He came to with a start and smiled at her. "Where did you say you were sent, with whom and for how long?" Jill had her finger in the page and flipped open the book.

CHAPTER 13

"In the autumn of 1940, when Hermann Goering's Luftwaffe shifted its bombing of England's aerodromes and radar stations to London, I was in West London with my parents and two brothers.

"Although we lived in the suburbs away from most target areas, errant bombs from the blitz began to make daily life dangerous.

"Even though my mother, two brothers and I slept in the new indoor shelter, a massive iron table taking up all the living space in the kitchen, life in London was becoming very hazardous. There was no room for my father beneath the table. So when not on Home Guard duty manning an anti-aircraft gun, he slept in the upstairs bedroom.

"Finally, Father told Mother, "The children have to get out of London. You must take them to your sister in the country, where they can stay until things get better here."

"Mother knew it had to be. She was comforted by his reminder that, unlike others, we were neither going to strangers nor too far away. (Many from high target areas had already been evacuated, some even going as far as Canada and the U.S., where they spent the duration of the war separated from their families.)

"We were as reluctant to go far from our parents as my mother was to let us go, especially when we learned that she would return to London. Besides, nine year old Peter and I, two years younger, rather enjoyed the wartime atmosphere. In the quiet and safety of the countryside we would be unable to search for shrapnel on our way to school after a night's raid.

"We couldn't listen for the wailing siren signaling us to troop from our classrooms to the shelters. With neatly-boxed gas masks slung across our chests, how we school children would sing our hearts out—'Somewhere Over the Rainbow' a favourite—until the all-clear returned us to our lessons.

Jill paused in her reading. "Well, Horst, that answers the where and the with whom questions. As for the how long, well, I remembered being in the country for an eternity, so was very surprised to find out years later that it was only for six weeks! Well, let's continue."

"Mother took us by train to the country and left us tearfully with Auntie Evie, who was already burdened with four young sons, one of whom, a spastic, required attention.

"As the only girl, and older, too, I soon became Auntie's daughter and helper. They were all handsome, bonny boys with tawny curls, obviously inherited from the Fields, as evidenced from the few straight black strands left on Uncle's bald head. Since he spent much of his time in his office, we didn't see much of him. When he returned, we were all abed or out of sight, for we knew that he ruled the house with a rod of iron. Known for his temper and impatience with children, we learned never to be around, especially if he had lost a legal case.

"It was summertime and I recall not one day's rain the whole time we were there. The big wooden rain barrel remained half-full the whole summer. Busy bees buzzed among the flowers which filled the country garden, beyond which lay miles and miles of fields with a few barns in the distance. A gate from the garden opened onto a path that led straight ahead and on around the cornfield to another field with a stile, where dwelt the bull; then another gate and stile until the path reached the road. Failure to close a gate behind us resulted in complaints from the angry farmer, or, far worse, a snorting bull on our tails! We could have taken a longer, safer, more boring route to get to town, but the way through the back garden, although hazardous, was shorter and more adventurous.

"How Peter and I hated going to that country school where we were the despised city children, and, at that, evacuees. We had to tolerate daily teasings and taunts from the smaller children and bullying from the older ones. Any day that we didn't have to go to school to face, first, the black beady-eyed bull and second, the big bullies, we were glad to stay with Auntie and her brood.

"Whenever a letter came from our parents, Auntie would read us tidbits and give us their love. The first letter contained the exciting news of the night we left London.

"As Father was home and alone, he had slept under the iron table." Jill paused. 'That's the iron table called an Anderson shelter that we slept under every night, Horst," she explained 'It was under this table that I would lie awake listening to the rat-a-tat of the guns and the rattle of Mother's sewing machine on the table top above. That reminds me. Mother's family on both sides were great seamstresses. Some were professional dressmakers with one uncle a royal tailor to European courts. Just another titbit of family history'

"As Father was home and alone, he had slept under the iron table," repeated Jill. "The house opposite was demolished by a direct hit. All our windows were shattered and the upstairs ceilings caved in, crashing down in clouds of plaster, beams and dust.

"Were it not for the table, Father would surely have been buried alive, if not killed outright. The blast from that night did, however, kill a neighbour who was shaving with an open razor. The blast jolted his arm and he cut his own throat! His name was surely on that bomb

"That reminds me, again. Grandma Field, who was doing her six months stint with us at the time was, even if there'd been room to squeeze in, unable to get underneath the table. This proud, sorrowed woman who sat in the darkness of her blindness while endeavouring to maintain her businesses despite her son's double dealings, refused to protect herself in any way from the dangers of the bombs.

"Until our departure for the country, our side of London, the more rural west side, had been somewhat spared as compared to the docks of East London which were attacked and devastated nightly. So it was usually a mis-directed bomb or haphazard dropping that caught us. On such air-raid nights we would throw on our dressing gowns and rush out to watch the magnificent sight of houses engulfed in flames come crashing and roaring to the ground in a heap of hot, seething embers. We only had one incendiary bomb hit our house. Father, wearing his tin hat, dashed up a ladder to the roof and quickly squirted water on it to extinguish the flames.

Horst smiled, remembering his own air-raid account. He urged her to continue her evacuation story.

"I was very homesick and cried at night. Peter and I shared a bed and I received little sympathy from him. I knew he was unhappy too, but being a boy knew better than to show his feelings. I devoted myself to my young cousins, especially the spastic one with the lolling head of curls and lopsided smile, whom I tenderly fed and cradled in my arms. Fate had decreed that Auntie Evie whereas she was incompatible with her first husband, had brought into the union with her second, an incompatability of blood. That, coupled with a fall down the stairs, resulted in the brain-damaged child. Their fifth and last child, the long-awaited daughter, was saved by modern medical knowledge and blood transfusions at birth.

"How I missed my parents and my home in London. But it still wasn't safe to return. Auntie seemed to be coping well for we were all happy enough and she loved us all. Her house was always one big mess of babies, bibs, potties, crumbs, crockery and washing, all confined to the back room that led onto the garden. The front room was for best, visitors and Uncle.

"On Sunday, however, the folding doors would be opened up and the dining room table extended around which five baby boys, Peter and I, Auntie and Uncle, were all seated for the Sunday roast. This was quite a formal occasion that brought us all together once a week.

"I remember one such Sunday when we had strawberries from the garden. Peter had greedily gobbled up all of his, while I was slowly sampling mine. I started with the smallest and saved the biggest, the reddest and the juiciest until the last, savouring the moment when I would slowly devour it. Suddenly, to my utter dismay, Peter's hand shot across to my plate, grabbed the luscious strawberry and popped it into his mouth. A sadistic grin spread over his face. One up on that little sister! I could do nothing but learn a bitter lesson that day, to be wary of people, especially an older brother, and never, ever flaunt one's precious possessions in anyone's face.

Then one day a letter came saying that Father was arriving to take one of us home with him. Who would it be? I had to be the one.

Father arrived by train on a Sunday. After the big midday meal in the best room, he suggested that he, Peter and I go for a bicycle ride during which he would tell us of their decision. We cycled a long way and I thought he would never speak. Finally he beckoned us to stop a couple of miles from the house.

"Your mother and I want all three of you back, but it's still not safe enough. One of you, anyhow, is going back with me." He took my brother aside and spoke briefly to him. Neither face told me anything. Then Father came to me and said, his hand on my shoulder, "Your mother wants you back most of all." My heart leapt! "But we decided it must be your younger brother. He's really too much for your aunt to handle along with her own." Father had tried to make the letdown as gentle as possible. The ride back and the packing up were painful. Then to watch cheerful Junior, to whom it meant nothing at all to be the chosen one, wave as he left with Father, was a terrible moment as I was left behind."

"Eventually, the Luftwaffe failed to crush the Royal Air Force and to break the British spirit. This meant that the chance of invading England had faded. Even though the blitz continued, Peter and I returned to London shortly afterwards.

"We were so happy to be home. Nothing much had changed. The bomb sites now sprouted tall purple weeks among the rubble, over which we clambered in our adventure games among the burnt exposed beams of the demolished rooms, the cracked bath tubs and toilets and the broken chimney stacks standing tall like silent sentries—and best of all, our endless search for unusual pieces of shrapnel to swap or add to our collection."

Jill put the book down with a sigh. "I felt it all over again," she said softly, "that awful empty feeling, as if it were yesterday, and then that wonderful feeling of coming home."

Horst was silent for a moment. "I know what you mean, Jillchen? I was hanging on your every word waiting to learn who went home. And the story of your father's survival under the table. Guess you'd call it Fate?"

"Fate, indeed. I also felt that I was doing 'my bit' again. In fact, I now remember that to my young mind our evacuation became a noble sacrifice which made our enforced absence from our parents easier to bear."

In a more cheerful tone, she waved the little flag and said "Long live the table! And what do you have to say to that, Horst? Any more stories from you?" she asked, thrilled that her decision to get him to talk about his past to give oomph to her own book, had already surpassed her wildest dreams.

"If not. Here's a riddle and one of my glib essays. See if you can guess the answer before I tell you!"

CHAPTER 14

"Riddle-me-ree! Riddle-me-ree! What do you get when you combine one pair of grandparents who produce three sons and four daughters, the oldest of the consecutive girls being my mother—with a second couple who begat nine children, the youngest of the three boys being my father—which from the total issue came forth twenty-six grandchildren, one of whom is me?

"Is this one of those trick questions? asked Horst, warily. Jill ignored him.

Now," she continued, "that makes in all twenty-six minus one as I'm on both sides—less my three brothers, already counted, which leaves…Now, let me see, x plus y divided by the number first thought of, multiplied by the lesser of the two evils, leaves me with a confused mess, a heck of a lot of cousins and relatives, not counting the ones first, second and once removed. The answer is a humongous pile of memories!" Horst groaned. "I know what's coming next! Alright, let's hear them."

"The entire blame, of course, for this generous bequest of close relatives and magnificent memories—all most memorable, some marvelous, others murky— bestowed upon me, lies strictly with Mother and her three younger sisters, all of whom stayed and stuck together in friendship and proximity when and wherever possible. Through all the thicks and thins of childhood, adult lives and twilight years—of family disputes, marital split-ups and pre, interim and post wartime endurances.

"The Four Graces! Wise, compassionate, long-suffering and proud! Mischievous, fun-loving, enmeshing in entangled situations, and builders of impossible dreams. Sweet, saintly, kind and stubborn! Slim, smart and sharp!

All beautiful women, Ivy, Evelyn (Evie), Vivien (Bibbie) and Olive (Lollie)—the Field girls.

"Ivy and Evie, a year apart, formed a team at the tender ages of three and four when sent away to a convent boarding school to be cared for by nuns while my grandmother was coping with the arrival of a new baby every year.

Jill turned to Horst. "I've never been able to fathom why those two little girls were sent away. The family was not at all hard up, even though Grandpa complained that the extravagance of his wife would one day ruin him. I know Grandma helped him in the shop, but they also had a nursemaid. Mother always said that it was when the fourth baby arrived and her mother needed rest, or something like that—but to send your children away! I just don't know." Her voice trailed off.

"Well," she continued reading, "although the nuns were kind enough to Ivy and Evie who often went home on the occasional weekend, they were also strict and prudish. Prudish in as much that in the bathtub those babies were draped in a huge white cloth so that neither they nor the nuns be offended at their naked bodies! And strict because they were discouraged to show their emotions.

Her voice was soft and low, as if talking to herself. "To this day I have yet to see Mother shed real tears. All she ever allows herself to do in times of distress is to lower her head to her chest, cover her eyes and give a momentary sigh. In a flash, she is again upright and calm.

Horst had a question. "Was the oldest child, the son, also sent away?"

"No, he was not," Jill answered vehemently. "Only the two little girls. That must have been the beginning of Mother's protectiveness and patience towards her younger mischievous sister. Their closeness lasted a lifetime.

She resumed reading. "We were the first of the large flock, my older brother, Peter, and I. We were the forerunners of a large race of siblings and cousins who arrived pell-mell over the World War years 1939-1945 as the result, either by accident or design, of a rash of conceptions and births to our own parents and their many siblings. Had Father's family of nine been as prolific, or as close in contact and homes as was Mother's of seven, we would, indeed, have been the role models and leaders of a much larger team. Our two-some divided only when Peter went eagerly on his own independent adolescent way, relieved at long last to leave us all behind.

"I, being closer in age and female, was more fortunate—or not, as the case may be, depending on one's viewpoint—to close ranks with my younger siblings and cousins as playmate, mentor, baby-sitter, peer and surrogate mother.

"I remember the night my brother Christopher was born. He's ten years my junior and was supposed to have been a sister for me. That would have evened up the gender statistics of two and two. It would also have given extra moral support to 'we two women among all those men' as Mother was wont to whisper to me. It encouraged us to stick together whenever she had had enough of her all-male family's pompous feelings of being the 'Lords of Creation'. I think Mother was one of the very first to feel the flutterings of Women's Lib and equality of opportunity for women, which was to come to fruition in the Seventies.

"Mother had even selected Cheryl, instead of Christopher, to go well with the name of Martin. I doubt she ever considered another boy, although she had considered Garth, after the big blond hero of a current comic strip, an apt name after all) and also Martin to precede the same surname--undoubtedly never thinking she would have to use either. For a quick decision Christopher was certainly a better choice. It blended in well with the saints' names of her other two sons, Peter and Michael. There's nothing saintly about my name. As I told you before, I was named after a popular musical running in London 'Jill Darling' at the time. Guess I wasn't worthy of a saint's name!

"Christopher, or his nickname Toffee, formed from his frustrated attempts to pronounce his name, was born at home in my parent's upstairs bedroom in the London suburb of Chiswick. It was a common practice for subsequent births following uncomplicated ones to be delivered by midwife at home.

"To get us out of the house on the night of his arrival, my brothers and I were sent down the road to sleep in Auntie Bibbie's house three doors away. When the news came late that night, I remember jumping up and down on the bouncy mattresses with my three younger girl cousins, as we cheered the new brother.

"I wouldn't have been quite so thrilled had I known what a little terror he was going to be and how he soon learned to twist Mother around his little finger—and that I would become his little mother for many years to come.

"We had our funny moments, too. One evening when Peter was oddly not in a bullying mood or plotting new tortures-(how I dreaded being left alone with him to baby-sit)—we were minding Junior and baby Chris. Our noses soon told us that baby Chris was in desperate need of a nappy change.

"Since neither Peter nor I could face the task, we sought out our gasmasks stored under the stairs, and put them on. With blurred vision and noses protected from the noxious smell, we accomplished the act, laughing nonstop while baby Chris roared his head off!

"Yes, we still had those gasmasks. It was 1945 and the war had only just ended. When I think of those gasmasks which we often had to don for practice, but, fortunately never for real, I remember the hateful smell of the suffocating rubber and the weird grunts of our breathing through the snout. Junior's gasmask was a brightly coloured Mickey Mouse face. Mine was an ugly , adult black one, and I was only six years old!

"Alright, Horst," said Jill, turning to her husband. She had a steno pad on her lap with pencil in hand. "Carry on. I'm taking down notes as you speak to record your family history for posterity."

Horst, who had wondered what she'd been scribbling down during his reminiscences, had his counter story ready.

"My father was the oldest of his family and my mother the youngest of hers. All were of good, solid German Protestant stock of the northern Germanic tribes. It was only when we moved to the southwest part of Germany that the family inherited some of fun-loving, easy-going ways of the tribes of that area.

Jill interrupted. "So Hitler's integration plan worked both ways, didn't it? The rigid Prussian disciplinary way of life developed a lighter side."

"Hmm, yes," But there's no riddle or algebraic nonsense in my family at all. It's all very straightforward. Two plus two equals four. Two sets of grandparents produced four children, each consisting of one son and one daughter.

"I am the oldest son of four, with two sisters and a younger brother. He's ten years younger and we were all born, raised and are still living in Germany, except for me.

"My mother's brother had four children and my father's sister, after many years of waiting, had an only son. I should have in all a total of five cousins, but one died, so that leaves four.

"My uncle on my mother's side and his wife lost their oldest son who died of pneumonia in his late twenties. He was living a bachelor life in West Berlin shortly after the construction in 1962 of the dreadful Wall that divided Germany and East and West Berlin in half. He lived only two hours away by car along the one highway through the East zone of Germany from his parent's home in the West. One winter he neglected a bad cold, dismissing it as unimportant. A week later, rushed too late to the hospital, he died an untimely, lonely death. Even modern medicine was useless. It was too late!

"His mother, my aunt, was devastated. Long had she nurtured him and her other children and brought them safely through the long, bitter war, only to have him snatched away from a promising future and happy life before him."

Jill remembered the cousin well for she had met him on a family visit to Germany many years before. She had a photo in their family album of the young man showing her young sons how to take aim with a rifle.

When Jill turned to the next section of her book, a brightly coloured leaflet lay between the pages—a knitting pattern. "Aha, that brings me to the clan of cousins. We grew up together and came through the war together. And I was Miss Bossy Boots."

CHAPTER 15

"Portrayed on the cover of a knitting pattern is a pair of brash youngsters, Tweedledum and Tweedledee, one a girl child with orange curls and the other a boy with brown pudding-bowl hair style. Two plump, hand-in-hand, fat-cheeked, unblinking Kewpie dolls clad in current knits for kids appear startled by the camera flash as they earn pin money for the sisters. Junior, my brother, and Barbara, Auntie Bibbie's oldest, were twin souls and close in age, interests, personalities, size and shape, as evidenced on the cover of the knitting pattern.

"My brother, Junior, (born on Father's birthday and named Reginald Michael, later known as Mike) was a dreamer and an idealist who with a bit of money in his pocket would have built a retreat for anyone with a hard luck story. Neither academically inclined nor sports-minded and whose personality was compatible to Fathers, he was the natural selection to work with him behind the counter of the inherited off-licence shop. In his thirties, Junior's straight brown hair receded on top and sprouted below as a curly gray beard studded with auburn."

Jill turned to Horst, "There's Grandma Field's reddish hair again, popped up in Mike's beard, and later his oldest daughter; cousin Barbara, and later her son, and way down the line in one of Auntie Evie's granddaughters. I do wish I could have seen Grandma Field's long golden locks. The little wisp cut off by Grandpa hardly does it justice!"

"In his teens Mike grew tall and thin. A soft-spoken boy with a shy smile, he attempted to perfect his fondness for music by playing the saxophone, guitar, cello and, of course, the piano, as did we all."

"Mother insisted on piano lessons to uncover any hidden ability or latent talent. How disheartened she became when none of us showed signs of serious study or inspired playing. I did learn to read music, despite the horrid piano teacher to whom I crept weekly to perform my unpractised scales and unlearned piece. Yet, I do remember practicing hard enough to play Percy Grainger's 'In a Country Garden' to the satisfaction of Grandma Field who was living with us at the time. I wasn't good enough to sight read or be an accompanist like Mother. But then I wasn't as bad as one of Evie's sons who, as the piano teacher arrived at the front door, would leave by the window!"

Horst laughed. "That story sounds familiar. You said something earlier in your book about his mother—and your mother—beating a hasty retreat through a window?"

"Good memory," Returning to the book, she read: "How the four Field sisters stuck together whenever and wherever possible. There were at least two at a time with their families living down the same road. When Auntie Evie lived in Stony Stratford where we were evacuated, the other three sisters lived within a few houses of each other in the London suburb of Chiswick.

"The movement between our three houses was non-stop. The beaten track in the front was as well-trodden as the narrow path between the back gardens and the tennis courts. Mother and her sisters were constantly on the borrow from each other and a fair exchange of items was always being exercised— kitchen utensils, condiments, children, toddlers, babies—and me, the babysitter and errand girl.

"Pop down to the butchers. I need something at the Co-op. Here's the dividend number. Get some things for your aunts as well. Don't forget the ration books and buy streaky bacon, not the back. It's too expensive. And don't for heavens sake break the eggs! We only get one each a week, anyhow!

"Do let the younger children go with you. I know they're slow, but it would help me a lot to get them off my hands for a while. Daddy will be home soon and I have to get his supper ready, otherwise he'll be like a bear with a sore head. Remember to feed your man first, then ask the favour! Off with you now. You can buy two ounces of sweets as a treat. There's one coupon left.

The many days I would be persuaded to pile up the perambulator with babies, young cousins, inside and out, hanging onto the handle, laden with blankets to sit, refreshments and money for ice cream to fill us. Should I show any sign of rebellion, the promised bribe that I could include the new puppies in the pram load, invariably changed my mind! We'd had a long succession of family dogs from Jim-ever-on-the-prowl mongrel to Judy-always-on-heat, a parade of sweet-natured spaniels and a couple of excitable poodles.

"Off to the park with all of you now. Don't come back before five and don't talk to any strangers! Yes, you will go, Pat, and you will do what your big cousin says. She's in charge! Put the babies in the pram, the two youngest hold onto the handle on either side and the bigger two hold on to their hands tightly! Don't let go and be careful crossing the road!

"Such a caravan would set off for a day in Chiswick Park, a beautiful former stately home, Burlington House. About a mile from our homes, it had extensive grounds with lakes, Italian gardens and a magnificent mansion.

"We'd go through suburban streets and alley ways, past the recreation ground or rec (I always looked for and never found a maritime disaster) with its busy slides and rocking seesaws, past the allotments with grinning scarecrows and digging for victory gardeners in their hobnailed boots. Across the busy roundabout with its honking cars, past derelict bomb sites, blasted buildings and schools with boarded up windows or empty spaces. Finally we would reach the brick wall of the park with its tall, wrought-iron gates. Once inside we'd aim for the grassy slopes down which we rolled, fed the ducks at the lake, play on the lawn, hide in the bushes and, if the park keeper didn't catch us first, swing on the low branches of the towering elms.

"Bibbie and Jack's middle daughter, Pat, with her dark hair cut straight and square, and I were always at loggerheads. I would spitefully call her Fatty or Jappy because of her small black eyes, chubby face and dark, straight bobbed hair (an insult in those wartime days especially after the bombing of Pearl Harbour.) That was my way of retaliating against her delight in reporting any unfavourable comments about me she'd overheard in the sisters' conversations. It was she, too, I know, who told on my Tell and Show games during which I would instruct any cousin, friend or neighbour child in the mysteries of the birds and the bees. I had surreptitiously gleaned the facts from Mother's medical encyclopedia, overheard grownup whisperings or heard the blatant words and crude signs imparted by peers in the park. Although I was temporarily disgraced and my position of trust waver a while, it was soon all forgotten by everyone but me, who was guiltily left with a lot of unanswered questions!

"Pat's assertiveness piqued my authority and upset my supreme command of the daily doings of the younger brood. It would be only many, many years later that we became friendly and like each other, long after clever Pat had gone onto University and become a teacher of mathematics.

"Valerie, the youngest of Bibbie's daughters, with the brown wavy hair and cornflower blue eyes, was compliant and sweet. She too, as did all the cousins, had a stint as fashion models. Frail and delicate, as a six week old baby she modeled a lacy Christening shawl for a knitting pattern. In her mid teens Valerie became the leader of the flock which I had left behind, organizing parties and dreaming up escapades for her band of siblings and cousins. She also became a favourite with my brother Peter's circle of men-about-town friends. She too, many years in the future, became the sole owner of the last of the five Field stores!

"A well-remembered and oft-sung ditty of those days 'The Campbells are Coming, Hurrah, Hurrah.' This became the doleful refrain "The Smiths are Coming, Beware, Boo-Hoo' whenever we heard of Auntie Evie's with sons impending arrival on one of her hasty retreats to London for brief respite from our uncle and her busy home in the country.

"We girls became thrillingly terror-struck at our darling dolls' perilous plight of sadistic abuse at the hands of her boisterous boys. Hurrah, hurrah would chant my brothers and boy cousins at the approaching reinforcements.

"Father's face would drop as he envisioned his sacred home and sanctuary being invaded by babies on potties, his tidy garden and lush lawn taken over and trampled on by noisy, wild boy children. Mother always staunchly defended her favourite wayward sister, who, she would hushedly hint at, was in need of rest and recuperation.

"The baby-sitting service I provided was, of course, a huge boon to Mother and Father, who delighted at the chance either to escape to the Moores, Auntie Lollie and Uncle Spence, for an evening of Bridge or escape to another world at the local cinema.

"Auntie Lollie, the slim sister with the straight fair hair, sharp fashion sense and tongue to match, was an immaculate housekeeper and a skillful knitter. Her husband, dashing Uncle Spence (with whom I share a birthday) had dark, wavy hair and a big handsome nose. He was a tennis fiend, a Francophile and the owner of a successful builder's merchants store in West London, that boomed in England's postwar re-building.

"He and Auntie waited five years until their first child was born. David, a flaxen wavy hair boy was followed three years later by a daughter, Maureen, who inherited her mother's uncurling hair. Until my two cousins were born, Auntie and Uncle were especially fond of my brother Peter and me. Even afterwards, we were still the recipients of the expert results of her clicking needles.

"Auntie Lollie continued knitting for many years until a painful skin rash caused by the new enzyme soap powders of the Sixties along with the dreaded arthritis immobilized those talented hands. Every stitch seemed to me to be a love stitch, as if those flying fingers fulfilled her body and soul.

"Run down to Auntie Lollie and ask her what time they'll be in for Bridge tonight and see if she wants you to baby-sit," was a repeated request of Mothers. No telephone in those days. Only Grandma Field had the necessary clout in her blindness and the ready funds to have one installed by her bedside to connect with her businesses.

"Down the road I'd skip to Auntie's upstairs flat and knock very politely to be admitted to the spotless living room with its large modern dining table, adorned with a tassled runner of green silk across its mirrored surface. Dead center sat an exquisite pot of paper-thin porcelain flowers which I admired and enjoyed touching the cold smoothness of its pastel petals. How I'd gaze at my two cousins' smart school uniforms and wonder how they stayed so immaculate, then to look at what Auntie was currently knitting; to end up clasping my arms gently around the huge furry body, smelling doggy and damp, of their pedigree Keeschond canine, Gelda. Everything about this aunt was pure pedigree!

"I was in charge of my three little girl cousins, their baby brother and my own younger brothers. We did a lot of growing up together. Auntie Lollie usually preferred that David and Maureen stay home, thinking, quite rightly so, that two extra children would be too much for me to manage. They later would have the undivided attention of a live-in French au pair girl who doubled her duties as French teacher to Uncle Spence.

"Auntie Bibbie was a quiet sweet-tempered Field girl, though known to flare up and put her foot down on occasions. She disliked quarrels, disputes and housekeeping. She allowed me to turn her upstairs attic room into a theatre and her children into performers. She made the best fruit cakes, light, golden soft and crumbly with the sultanas and raisins evenly distributed, (so unlike Mother's hard, over-baked and burnt.) This auntie always showed an interest in me as a young child, and as a growing girl would seem to understand when I had a private sorrow.

"With my hand around the back door, younger brother clinging around my knees and my arms tightly around baby brother, I would ask Auntie Bibbie, busy in her kitchen vainly attempting to get her home in order and meals on the table, 'May I come and play with the girls? I've got a new play I want to rehearse them in upstairs.'

"The oldest daughter with the golden curls, the dark-haired outspoken middle young miss and the youngest with the brilliant blue eyes were either dressed alike in home-made dresses of crisp cotton or in their colour preference of blue, pink and green. With the baby boy we would hustle up to the attic where I put them through their paces and direct them indefatigably until our show was ready for the eyes and ears of an audience. Our mothers, aunts and neighbours welcomed the opportunity to meet with each other, gossip during and applaud after the unseen performance!

"Auntie Bibbie's husband, dear Uncle Jack, a favourite uncle with his tall war stories, was a wiry, wisecracking former London bus driver (a no-no to mention, for had he not married into the Field First Family!)

"Uncle Jack, tell us again how many Germans you shot during the war," we'd all plead, unknowing that during his call-up he had never gone beyond English shores. Anticipating his pantomiming expertise of shooting down all the Hun, with fingers held horizontally beneath our noses and arms extended in a Heil Hitler salute, we'd strut around shrieking with laughter and fear as Uncle chased us with his imaginary rifle, rat-a-tat-a-tat-ing!

"To entertain and frighten us further he'd dislodge his false teeth into the front of his mouth, roar threateningly, grimace and roll his eyes as he menacingly grabbed at us. Then to stop suddenly, smile with his teeth back in his mouth, roar with laughter and reach into his pocket to bring out a few coins that he'd toss to me and tell me to take the whole brood off to buy some ice-cream cones.

"Down through the narrow winding alley with its high enclosing walls of gray brick backing onto small, mean backyards; along to rough Devonshire Road, the scene of Saturday night brawls and Chiswick's low life, to the ice cream shop, to buy three penny cornets of the one and only vanilla flavour, soft, creamy and swirling. With bibs on the babies and sticky fingers licked and wiped all the way home, we would drag our feet so as not to arrive home too soon. Our parents needed their aloneness, rest and respite from the constant noise and presence of so many youngsters!

"Although Auntie Bibbie always said that she enjoyed her three girls and that parents accepted and loved any baby regardless of its gender, they were overjoyed when their fourth child, John, born during the last year of the war was the longed-for son. He was a year older than my youngest brother, Chris. Being so close in age and homes, both boys grew up as brothers, and I was the awful older sister. How I would despise them as I watched them cruelly behead ants, de-wing flies and slice up worms!

"Christopher was a true Field, big, blond, forthright, astute and demanding. The photo portrait of Grandpa Field is a replica of Chris as he is today. John, canny like his East Londoner father, was a good match for my baby brother. Both would at one time enter the family businesses, only to depart—one in a hasty retreat and the other in a nasty temper!

Horst despaired. "Not another riddle, Jill.

Jill smiled. "No, not a riddle, but here's a rhyme just popped into my head."

> *Children no longer for all are grown*
> *Long, long departed from parent's home*
> *Though many stayed close, a few did roam*
> *But all have made it on their own!*

"Regarding the 'riddle' statement, both Chris and John went their own separate ways."

"Hmmm," said Horst thoughtfully, thinking that didn't explain anything at all. He let it pass, eager to continue with his own story. Jill's long discourse and millions of memories of her wartime growing up with such a large family had jogged his own memory.

He was still in the midst of the war, evacuated with his mother and sisters, and oblivious to the fact that the end was in sight. Tough times lay ahead, They had no friends or family support, so unlike his wife's seemingly pleasant life on the other side of the English Channel!

"Well," said Jill, flourishing a pencil. "I'm ready with my pencil and pad again to jot down in shorthand as you speak." He paused and looked at Jill, who from the expression on her face, had come up with the same sudden idea.

They chorused. "We'll use the tape recorder." Why hadn't they thought of that before. Horst went down the stairs to their bedroom and retrieved the little machine they'd brought to tape family messages.

"I'll put in a new tape and then we're all set to go."

Jill was delighted with the instant recording. She'd worried that she'd have trouble transcribing her shorthand scribbles!

CHAPTER 16

"Here it is, Jillchen. All set up and ready to go," said Horst, sitting back down on the top stair. He held the microphone to his lips and began his story.

"In November 1944 Mama went to the nearest hospital in the spa town of Bad Durkheim, famous for its underwater mineral waters and gambling casino, and the famous Wurstmarkt or Wine Festival. Of course, none of these were in operation during the war. Mama gave birth to my brother.

"She was very fortunate to be accepted into a hospital at that time as every facility was used for the war-wounded and the dying, or for the fortunate members and their families of the Nazi party. Papa's position was too low down in the Party echelon, yet he managed to arrange it through his position with the Police Force.

"During the war every young girl between the ages of 16 and 22 was ordered as part of her education to work in a home as a mother's help and nursemaid.

"When Mama went into hospital we had as our helper a young girl from our home town. I remember this silly girl over-indulging on the abundance of grapes growing in our area, the Pfalz or Palatinate wine-growing region. After stuffing herself with grapes, she then consumed gallons of water. When her belly swelled up, she was rushed, screaming in pain, to Emergency where she had her stomach pumped out!

"We also had one other helper, a Polish girl brought into Germany as forced labour from occupied Poland. Unable to speak any German, and we knowing no Polish, our only means of communication was by using the word 'dobshe' which means 'good' in English. Everything was either 'No dobshe' or 'Yes dobshe' denoting favour or disfavour, accompanied with either a smile or a frown. It would have been easier communicating with a dog.

"Out of the question, however, was a family pet. Living as we did in an apartment, the usual custom in Germany, very few people kept dogs. The only ones I saw were savage guard dogs chained up at local farms, or the many magnificent German Shepherd dogs, or Schaefer Hunds, in partnership with the police. And," Horst said, turning to his wife. "You know that our name Schaefer means a shepherd in German, so a Schaefer Hund originally helped shepherds herd the sheep.

"Well," he continued, "In the winter of 1944 we had a heavy snowfall. Mama went on one of her shopping trips, with me, to the next village and decided to wear her warm black fur coat.

"Only a short way from the house, just as we were crossing an open field to enter the woods, suddenly enemy planes loomed in the sky above.

"I ran to the woods, but Mama couldn't run as fast. Visible in her dark coat against the white snow, she was a perfect target to the sniping planes. With the speed of lightening she dug herself into the snow and covered herself with as much of the cold white stuff to camouflage the blackness of her coat. The planes circles around, shot spasmodically at the road, then left. Mama remained dug in for at least half an hour, emerging only when she knew the planes had departed for good.

"We returned home. Mama was shivering from shock and cold. Her face was all shriveled up from the icy coldness of her protective tomb."

"What a story, Horst," said Jill, thinking to herself that she would regard her mother-in-law with added admiration from then on. "Bet she didn't go out in that coat in the snow ever again." Horst nodded and continued his story.

"In the spring of 1945 the distant air-raid noises were supplemented by the continuous rumble in the west. We learned they were the noises made by the Allied tanks as they slowly advanced into Germany. The main road from the Western Front to the River Rhein was finally blocked by American and English troops, forcing the remnants of the German army to retreat through our valley and by-passing the main traffic arteries.

"What a pitiful sight. There was the pride of German manhood walking slowly, dejectedly and ragged. Our band of boys picked up discarded rifles, binoculators, boots, ammunition and radios, that we wrapped in water-proof cloth and buried for later retrieval. The soldiers gave these articles away freely in exchange for a few dried-up potatoes. Amongst the last of the German troops retreating, one young, fresh-faced soldier said to me, 'You are very lucky not to have to march with us. Tomorrow you will have bread and chocolate! I wasn't quite sure what he meant.

"Rumours quickly spread throughout the village that the Americans would arrive any day. They were two-headed monsters who would rape the women, take our few last potatoes and shoot every male over ten. Mama's chief concern, however, was for our chickens. She decided to hide them. We cut air holes in some cardboard boxes, put the chickens inside and hid them in a corner of the kitchen.

"The day came. Rumble, rumble. The huge tanks came slowly around the corner of the valley. All the villagers had sacrificed their best white sheets by plastering them all over the houses as a sign of surrender. Mama, my two younger sisters, baby brother and myself, all waited in the kitchen, holding hands and frightened out of our wits.

"Curiosity got the better of me. I sneaked out of the house, ran across the meadow and hid by the side of the road waiting for the enemy. The first tank with its window slit in the turret was turning half left, half right, peering everywhere. I saw American soldiers sitting on the tanks. To my surprise they looked just like myself. They were not two-headed monsters! I ran back to report this to my dis-believing family.

"When the Americans had secured the valley road, they came into our small village. Dressed in smart, clean battle-fatigues and clean-shaven, they looked as if they had walked out of a magazine. They came to our house. A lieutenant knocked on the door, spoke in German and politely requested the living room for ten of his men to sleep in. Mama burst into tears and quickly answered 'Yes, of course'. What else could she say? The officer calmed her down and handed a bar of chocolate to us, the taste, smell and appearance of which I had long forgotten!

"Next morning our chickens began to cackle in the kitchen. One of the Americans came to Mama and asked for some eggs in exchange for a can of coffee. We watched him take the eggs, go into the bathroom, crack open the eggs and proceed to shampoo his hair! For days we were speechless at such extravagant behaviour and flagrant waste!

"The war moved away from us towards the River Rhein. A token ten men platoon remained in our village, who gradually became less and less friendly, formed their own groups and stopped mingling with the locals. We learned later that fraternization between Americans and Germans was not desired by the American military commanders.

"Food became very scarce. We lived on potatoes and wheat which we ground ourselves to make into some kind of bread.

"By 1946 Papa had been taken prisoner by the French and was in a camp in France for nearly four years." Horst slowly put down the microphone.

"Phew, grim days for you, Horstchen," consoled Jill, pausing a few moments before raising her voice to say, "But, the war was over and we were victorious." She cheered and waved the Union Jack.

"How we children would race around chanting 'We've won the war! We've won the war! We had Victory parties in the roads, victory parades down the streets." She pointed to a black and white photo taken outside the Chiswick homes showing a joyous group consisting of uniformed Uncle Jack surrounded by Auntie Bibbie and their four children, Auntie Lollie with David, snatched from his bed in pajamas, and Jill and Mike atop the de-railinged wall. "There was no more hissing and booing at Hitler on the cinema screen. He was dead. The Jerries were beaten!"

"Alright, alright," admonished Horst. "The Germans were defeated, and, true, we hadn't been able to cross the Channel to conquer England as we'd promised." He shot a quick glance at his wife. Jill knew what was coming. "But, ha, ha," he chortled, 'that was to come much later when I arrived!"

"Don't you be so cocksure, my man," murmured Jill under her breath. "No, nothing, lieb, no comment," she stalled, and to distract him, turned a page and pointed to a photo of a small group standing around a car.

Figure 1
The Martin residence with the attic

Figure 2
Field Stores in Hammersmith

Figure 3
The inherited Field Stores

Figure 4
Going to school in 1940

Figure 5
Mother and her children as magazine models

Figure 6
The Tweedledum and Tweedledee models

Figure 7
The dancing for the troops days

Figure 8
VE Day 8ᵗʰ May 1945

Figure 9
Dining in style
The Moores and the Martins

Figure 10
Ivy Field and Reginald Martin wedding 1931

Figure 11

Jill and Horst's wedding 1959

Figure 12

The Martin residence of Jill & Horst's wedding

Figure 13
Opa Schaar

Figure 14
Mama's Mutterkreuz (Mother's Cross)

Figure 15
Ludwigshafen bombed

Figure 16
The apartment building on Wittelsbachstrasse in Ludwigshafen

Figure 17
The air-raid bunker in Ludswigshafen

Figure 18
The River Rhine with its barges

Figure 19
Typical German apartment blocks huddled around courtyards

Figure 20
Mama and Papa Schaefer and family

Figure 21
Young Horst

Figure 22
Horst with sisters

Figure 23
Horst with boyfriends

Figure 24
The Big Barrel at Bad Durkheim

Figure 25
Hitler Youth poster

CHAPTER 17

"The war was long over, and time to enjoy life once again," explained Jill, pointing to the car in the photo.

"Brand new and a beautiful blue, it was the first visible sign of our newly acquired affluence. We had suddenly come up in the world after my mother and her three sisters became the beneficiaries of my grandmother's estate of three wine and spirit stores located in various parts of London. A surprise windfall was this indeed as everything had been willed to the three sons who, fatefully, one by one, predeceased my grandmother. After much haggling among the four sisters and their spouses over the equal division of four into three, my mother and father ended up with one small shop and a sum of money which enabled us immediately to rise up in the world and away to a better neighborhood, friends, schools and the purchase of all the accompanying accouterments and comforts of our new position – hence our first car.

"It's a lovely day," my father said. "We've had enough of keeping cool under the hose in the garden. We deserve a trip to the sea in the car." This was a long speech for my father, who eagerly studied the cloudless blue sky with a gleam in his eye as he anticipated mastering the car with his hand on the wheel and his foot on the pedal.

"As if previously prepared for such a sudden campaign, my mother had her troop of six quickly organized and packed into the car with all the necessities for an enjoyable day at the sea: buckets and spades for the beach brigade, paste and cress sandwiches and a Thermos of tea for the trusty officers. We set off eagerly for the two-hour trip from London to the coast. In the excitement of getting on our way, no one minded when pleading car sickness I asked to sit up front next to the driver. My brothers had forgotten the discomfort of a long journey squeezed like sardines in the back. Ensconced like a princess on her throne, I perched high on a pillow next to my father and contentedly watched the scenery slipping by from city to countryside, ever-changing, from chimney stacks and crowded dirty buildings to the wider open spaces of fresh air, thatched cottages and cows. I clung to every moment of such bliss for I knew it would not last.

"The intermittent silences of the baby sleeping, my mother dreaming and the boys engrossed in silent battle behind me, were interspersed with discontented mutterings that increased in volume and tempo as the car ate up the miles.

"We're almost there, boys," my mother said wearily for the umpteenth time, desperately attempting to divert their interest to the passing panorama.

"First one to see the sea gets sixpence." My father's offer aroused everyone's attention to the alertness and uprightness my mother had repeatedly tried to achieve. Unscrambling themselves to peer right, left and straight ahead over the seats, my brothers had little chance of winning the prize. I, from my high vantage point up front, had the first glimpse of the ocean as we rounded the corner of the High Street that led down the hill to the promenade.

"As soon as we had found a parking place on a grass verge close to the beach, unloaded everyone and everything from the car and set up camp, we began our enchanting day of sunshine and smiles. Yet. no sooner unleashed to discover a wonderful new world of sand, sea, shells, swimming and seaweed that we'd hear father announce, "Time to pack up and go. Hurry now, we have to beat the traffic."

"She's not sitting up front again," came the chorus of my brothers. "It's my turn. It's not fair." Mother, not about to be unseated again, sat up front with baby brother. Toppled off my throne, I was confined to the crush and cramp of the back where my brothers elbowed me into the left-over soggy sandwiches, damp towels, salty swimsuits and slimy seaweed. Left behind were the sand castles and sunny smiles as we joined the caterpillar of cars crawling along the dusty road.

"Shut inside the oppressive shell of the car, we inched our way along the highway that glinted silvery in the setting sun. Our car moved slowly bumper to bumper, stopping and starting, overtaking with a "hurrah" only to find that no head start had we gained. No use complaining about the state of my stomach and the pounding in my head. My parents were in the midst of a squabble.

"Are you sure I should have turned off back there?"

"No, you should have taken the turning before that."

"How can you expect me to turn off if you don't give me enough warning?"

"Tempers became heated; dislike steamed off the grimy windows. Thirsts went unquenched and tears undried as the trek home dragged on.

"I'm going to be sick," I gurgled between teeth clenched together in an effort to dam off the upsurging tide. My brothers fell away from me with a roar of disgust.

"Get to the window quickly," urged my mother. She handed me a towel while holding the slippery baby and shoving another brother aside to free the window for my face.

"Oh sweet release! I hung my head outside, eyes tightly closed as the breeze fanned my brow. The doleful journey continued amid the putrid odor of upset stomachs, unwashed sweat, unchanged baby, leaking oil, spilt gasoline and milk, my father's cigar, and my mother's futilely dabbed-on perfume.

"Many hours later, long after the sun had left us in the gloom, our weary band finally made its way up the driveway, vowing never again to leave home. But we knew we would---the next time the sun shone, faraway places beckoned, and father's foot itched!"

Horst loved the reading and told Jill what a vivid picture she'd painted of her family's outing. "Our postwar period was the beginning of some of our worse times," he said. "No trips to the seaside for us. Just getting back home to Ludwigshafen was trial enough!"

"Mama decided it was time to leave the village and return to Ludwigshafen. Since there was no transportation available, we took a hand cart loaded up with a few possessions, my two sisters and baby brother, and set out to walk to Ludwigshafen forty miles away. It was fortunately summertime, so with nights spent under the hedgerows, in ditches and the occasional ride in a truck, we accomplished the distance in two days.

"We arrived at our old apartment that had miraculously survived the bombs, although the roof was gone and two of our rooms were open to the sky. It had also been taken over by French soldiers who agreed to give us one of the roofless rooms. We put a canvas over it and spent the next six months there.

"The other tenants in the building were unkind to Mama because of Papa's arrest as a Nazi. They had also stolen some of her possessions from our bombed-out apartment. Mama could see them displayed on their balconies around her. They rationalized their behaviour by saying that the Nazi Schaefers did not deserve any possessions. They deserved to be punished. How many of them were actual Nazi sympathizers, I will never know, yet Papa in his official position was an obvious target.

"Food was now really scarce. We were rationed to three slices of bread and one potato a day. The French vacated our apartment and moved into billets next door in the big old school building. The American zone was across the River Rhein and life there was much better for those in that zone. The French seemed to be as poor as we were and it was in their zone, from the Rhein to the French border, in which we found ourselves. It was almost impossible to get a pass to go across the river to Mannheim, the American zone, where bread was more readily available.

"One day I walked up to the bridge where a big black soldier asked me for my pass. Since I could not produce one, he then asked me, 'You Nazi? You bad?' 'No,' I cried. He must have felt sorry for me for he allowed me to pass. With the few goods I had to use as barter, I was able to obtain some loaves of bread and returned home proudly.

"One of our survival procedures was to raid freight trains. The railroad tracks leading up to the Rhein Bridge were on a slope. A group of we boys would grease the rail tracks which caused the wheels of the locomotive to skip and the train to slow down. Crowds of people would board the train and throw down to the ground potatoes, cabbages and coal, all the while being shot at by the soldiers on the train.

"This was one of my daily tasks until I was caught one day by the French police. It was the shoes that did it—or lack of them. My feet were encased in large squares of felt gathered at the top around the ankles and stapled at the toes, which were supposed to make me fleet of foot. The only clothing available to purchase with ration cards was made of wood fibre. The only problem with this material was that it stretched when wet to twice its size. A very popular material was the flour sacks from the American Wheat programme. These Mama sewed and dyed into very durable outfits. I never had any problem with size as everything was made to measure.

"However, I was forced to take my sackful of bounty to the French police station and empty it onto the floor. I was slapped about a bit and told to clean the station floor. Then, with a smile, I was told to get out and not to get caught next time.

"Many coal thieves were being caught by the French police. One story goes that one thief was caught and beaten up. When asked in French if he wanted any more, he replied with the only French he knew. 'Oui, oui, oui.' So they beat him up some more. Again they asked him and again he replied 'Oui.' This was repeated until the police stopped and sent him on his way. Black and blue of face and body, when he met his friends next day, he told them that if he hadn't spoken such good French, they would have killed him!"

Jill gasped. "Oh, what problems a language can cause. Remember Papa and the Latin idioms I couldn't translate?"

"Speaking of Papa," said Horst, "there was no news of him. Our so-called friends and neighbours told us gleefully that as a former Nazi, he had surely been shot by then.

Jill put her arms around her husband. "Well, we know that wasn't true, don't we?

CHAPTER 18

The cardboard shoe box that had slipped from Jill's grasp on her precarious descent from the attic lay at Horst's side. The bold words 'Freeman, Hardy and Willis—good quality shoes for all the family' on the askew lid caught her attention. "And to think, Horst, that at that same time you were going through all those post-war problems, I was worrying about getting shoes and clothes to fit,." confessed Jill. "When Mother took me shopping for clothes, I always ended being sent from the Junior Miss department—I was only fourteen, but tall and skinny-- to the Outsize Women's department. All the matronly clothes swamped me; only the hems were long enough. Finally, Mother, who had a mean way with the sewing machine, made most of my clothes. At least they fit, and from an economic viewpoint she was able to buy more material and make more outfits with the allotted clothing coupons."

"These were our days of austerity, liebling," she explained. "Although we'd been the victors in the war already five years behind us, everything was still rationed—nothing as bad as your situation—but, food, sweets, clothing and petrol." She grimaced and added, "Only the nasty-tasting cod liver oil was plentiful and unrationed, and fortunately concentrated orange juice for infants and babies."

"And as for getting the right shoes for school to fit my long, narrow feet, I wrote right here in the book," she said with a laugh, "I'd whisper my size to assistant who eyed me as some sort of freak and say 'Sorry, we don't carry anything that large.'

"Trying to get suitable school uniform shoes--brown, flat-heeled buttoned with a T-strap for indoors and lace-ups for outdoor wear—was an ordeal for

Mother. She had the same problem with my tall, skinny brother Peter with large feet, too. She resorted to adding inches to sleeves and letting down trouser legs while he squeezed into the largest shoe size available."

Turning to her husband, she said, "Those Big and Tall shops that came later—in Germany, too—I bet, Horst, were unheard of until later generations grew taller bodies and bigger feet!"

"One day," she continued, "after a futile search all over the West of London, Mother bought, the only shoes in my size--a pair of bright yellow and black tartan low-heeled shoes! To my mortification she then got special permission, pleading no doubt the trials and tribulations of clothing a giantess, for me to wear them as indoor school shoes. Among the dull uniformity of beiges, browns and navy blues, how those flashing shoes caught the attention of the entire school of 500 girls as I entered the assembly hall, even though I was doing some speedy footwork in an attempt to blur the brightness. How I wished for a hole to open up and swallow me whole, never again to emerge! But, the damage was done. So I dyed them brown to disguise their gaudiness. Of course everyone could see what I had tried to do. Perhaps it would have been better if I'd braved it out until the shoes wore out!"

She picked up a cardboard tube from among the fallen photos and pulled out a long narrow photo that uncoiled to reveal a black and white panoramic view of the 500 pupils of the Sacred Heart Convent High School for girls. "Here, Horst, hold on to the other end while I refer to my book," she ordered. "Look here," she said, pointing out rows of girls from nine to eighteen years of age, posed like peas in a pod with the nuns and teachers like big black beans in the center. "Want to hear about my long gone-by schooldays first, and then you can talk about yours into the recorder?" Horst nodded and listened as Jill read.

"Oh, those high school days at the Convent; a spiritual hideaway of cloisters with large-as-life medieval oil paintings; the echo of our slides on the red-tiled floors; contemplative singing nuns, some kneeling in prayer, others with hitched up habits on their knees polishing those floors to a slippery shine. Choking incense in the chapel; the smell of cabbage that wafted through the corridors into the classrooms to let us know was for lunch and long lingered after the awful taste; the little bottles of compulsory milk, freezing in winter and in summer warm and rancid.

"The high spirits and pungent scent of non-deodorized girls in serge uniforms, growing spiritually while giggling and praying in the chapel, academically from the long school days and nightly homework, and physically from natural feminine development and the compulsory games of netball, rounders, tennis and P.E.

"Girls with plaits and tied-back tidy hair disciplined by prefects who stood sternly on the stairs. Girls who stood to attention when a superior entered the room and curtseyed to Mother Superior. No talking in class, in assembly, in the cloakroom and speak only when spoken to, especially at mealtimes. Girls, rowdy upon leaving the school building, discarding the dreadful navy-blue berets with badge regardless of being spotted, reported and given an order mark˙ to bring down and disgrace the House to which each was assigned. To return to the world of familiar smells and sounds of families and everyday lives outside those wall. To change out of the drab, musty uniform into a pair of modern slacks, bright and comfortable.

"Nobody ever knew that I was an eloquent orator or articulate actress. I preferred to keep my mouth shut rather than express my views or impress with clever answers to difficult questions. It was too embarrassing to have the words stall in my throat or fumble and fall over each other in their desperation to express themselves. Mother was crestfallen that I wasn't the great actress she had always aspired to. She even gave me elocution lessons to help me along.

"Sport became my forte. Apart from being good enough to be on the school teams, it was comparatively effortless to rah, rah, rah at the end of a netball match or make the sporting handshake over the tennis net and say 'Well played'. I suppose being tall I was a natural for the shooting position on the netball team. I remember the proud moment when I was called to the stage at morning assembly before all 500 girls and staff to receive my school colours. This award was given for receiving three 'mentions' of good play in matches against other schools.

"I became captain of the Second Netball team after being demoted from the First Team. I'd turned up tardy and out of school uniform. It was a Saturday morning, a non-school day and I was rebellious against petty rules and teachers with 'pets'. The Games Mistress's pet got the place as shooter on the First Team while I was made captain of the Second. However, I enjoyed being a big fish in a small pond rather than the other way around.

"Tennis, too, was my game, although I never got my name on the coveted silver cup. I was points away from winning against a senior player. The entire school was cheering me on, when suddenly I allowed the 6th former to beat me. Perhaps I was unable to handle success and all the expectations that came with it. However, I was selected to play for the school and spent many a thrilling victorious time traveling the team to all the schools in and around London for 'away' matches.

"I was also in the hockey team as right wing. How I dreaded those freezing winter days on the icy field, garbed only in knee-length billowing, box-pleated shorts and flimsy open-necked cotton shirt. The Games Mistress, masculine Miss Bonser of my netball story, bundled up in thick coat, woolen scarf, warm mittens and fur boots and hat, ordered the players to strip down to shorts and shirts before play could commence.

"Waiting for the swift ball to come streaking out to me to retrieve, run with down the field, rush in past the big backs to shoot or pass to the screaming center forward for her to score the goal, I never minded how many bruised shins I got from hefty swings of those sticks against my shin pads or knocks on the head from rock hard flying balls—as long as I, waiting in the cold wings, was able to stop those first long drives without a fumble!

"Angela and I were best friends. How we'd get uncontrollable giggles in the chapel! How she'd hate it when I found a pipe-cleaner curler left in her nightly-tightly curled-up birds nest hair! A twin-some twosome were Angela and I until I sportingly invited a new girl, Barbara, to join us—and then we were three! Sometimes I'd be the gooseberry. Teamed up against me, they'd teasingly remind me that since I was two years their junior, they had secrets unsuitable for one of my tender years!

"We made a great trio as we practiced shooting into the net whenever we could, often completing a round of twelve shots from different positions without one miss. When I received a coveted all-leather netball for my birthday, the expensive ball never left my side. The one time I weakened and loaned it out, the borrower sent it soaring over the goalpost, over the brick wall of the school into the busy traffic outside—never to be seen again. Her pocket money, or her parent's equally hard-earned wages, bought me a new one. I inked my initials on the ball, turned deaf ears to entreaties, and kept the precious possession by my side at all times.

"Those school days began after I'd finished primary school two years early at age nine. A precocious, clever-for-her-age child with billowing curls (Mother had discarded the rag curlers to experiment with endless frizzy perms) all the girls thought I was a reincarnation of Shirley Temple. On my first day I was led on a long walk down an endless corridor by a huge creature in black robes to my new classroom of thirty eleven years olds. I was the only new girl, two years their junior, one term late and with a lot of catching up to do in French and Latin.

'Five years later, having completed my studies and passed all my exams, I discovered to my horror that the new School Leaving Act prevented my leaving school until I was sixteen. So I had to bide my time, a lovely two years in fact, as Head of the House, a prefect still bossing Bibbie's daughters, being adored by the little girls, studying what I chose, and creeping home early past the sleeping nun at the front door into the noisy bustle of the refreshing world outside. I also wore the Sixth Form uniform of skirt and pale blue woolen sweater, which much to my chagrin became shrunk, matted and colorless from Mother's inexpert washings. Poor Mother, who before her marriage had begged Grandma Field to teach her how to cook, only to be told 'Not in my kitchen. Make your own mistakes in yours'. Likewise the laundry. Knowing little about washing clothes, Mother resorted to stomping on a bath tubful of dirty clothes which she hung up unrinsed and dripping wet!"

Horst roared with laughter as Jill with a far-away look on her face as if still lost in her schooldays, slowly closed the book.

"How different my schooling was from yours," he said, raising his voice and coughing to get her attention. "Of course, you did go to a parochial school that seemed to offer a more select education."

"And," added Jill, "a segregated school, too. In fact, years later when I took evening classes I couldn't concentrate with males around. Today I'd opt for a coeducation system. But then I do feel that separating the sexes may have its advantages—although," she continued with a laugh as she rolled up the school photo and slid it back into its tube, " I can't quite put my finger on any right now." She turned to her husband. "Anyway, Horst, it's your turn again. Ready to tell me about your schooling after the war? He nodded, good and ready to go.

CHAPTER 19

"School started up again in earnest. Some of the teachers had been dismissed for accepting bribes of food and fuel in exchange for good grades. Whereas our instruction had only been spasmodic up till then, we started with six hours a day.

"All history ended just before the first World War. It was as if the Second World War had never happened. We in the French zone had to learn French. No excuses allowed. In fact, every street name was gradually changed into French. It looked so strange to see Ludwigsstrasse called Rue de Louis.

"The students remained in one classroom with the teachers rotating from room to room. There was one teacher for each subject. Having no electricity we were summoned by a bell rung by the headmaster and classes could only be held during daylight hours. Because the stairs had been completely demolished, the first and second floors could be reached only by a ladder propped up between each landing."

Jill interrupted. "Gracious me! In my school it was traditional to ring a bell even though we had electricity. Those ladders don't sound too safe, either. Ever have anyone fall down and drop all their books--just like I did today?" Horst shook his head and continued speaking into the microphone.

"Each classroom had a huge pot-bellied stove, kept burning during the cold winters. A practical joke was to put a piece of rubber on top of the stove and wait for it to melt. The resulting stink and smoke caused class to be dismissed for the day!

"American Quakers provided school meals for the students. We were provided with a metal dish with spoon clipped onto the lid. It was this dish we would hold out like little Oliver Twists, begging from the American field kitchens in the school yard next to our apartment building. A continual daily theme was the clank, clank, clank of metal scraped against metal, as the hundreds of students downed their daily meal as quickly as possible so they could rush up for seconds.

"One day a hefty boy pushed ahead of me in the food line. I, being the tallest, though thinnest, of all my shorter, swarthier Southern German friends (How I hated being called Lange or Lofty) was volunteered to challenge him. He laughed, and knowing that I would have to get him with my first blow, I hit out. My hand almost shattered. He staggered, then left, right, left, right, he rained blows to my head and body. I went down, dazed. I hadn't felt as bad since I fell down the stairwell when sliding down the banisters of our eight flights of stairs. All my teeth were loosened and I was unable to speak for three weeks."

"Ooh, there're those stairs again," commented Jill, horrified at the image of the young boy plunging down the eight flights of stairwell. "Carry on with the story, please."

"I was a good student. Learning came easily to me and I didn't have to study too much. One of the teachers I disliked, even hated. He was the teacher of our Physics class, my best subject, and had been injured as a paratrooper during the war. He was not considered a Nazi because of his celebrated war deeds, yet the ideas he proclaimed in class belied the fact. He had been shot in the throat, the bullet exiting behind his ear, which left him with his head lolling to one side at a 45 degree angle and slurred speech. Being only 5'3" tall and disfigured, he took an instant dislike to 6'5" me.

"I worked especially hard to please this teacher, doing extra research which when presented to him, would reply, 'Don't present such rot to me. Remember you are talking to a well known physicist.' Other boys, not so clever, were treated cordially.

"Thirty years later I was to meet this man again and he was unchanged. When I introduced myself to him, he curtly and impolitely said, 'So what!'

"I always had one best friend. One of them was Rudolph who lived in a two-bedroom apartment not far from me. He was one of five children, one of which was a mentally-retarded sister. This child was hidden during the war to escape Hitler's extermination programme of the mentally and physically defectives. Rudolph also foraged for his family. However, I chose not to go with him for he preferred going where the trains made their stops. I considered it too dangerous as there were too many guards around.

"Next was Gerhard, not quite my height and with dark curly hair. We were always in competition as to who would wear the most dashing costume during the pre-Lenten Carnival, or Mardi Gras—and always over girls, too!

"It was with Gerhard that I decided to escape the provinciality of Ludwigshafen. We decided to build a raft and float the hundreds of miles downstream to Holland at the end of the Rhein. With eight tires bound together and topped with planks of wood, we loaded up the raft with food and set off. At the first bridge we bumped into the support. The tires burst and it was the end of our journey.

"Then there was Herman, a short, stocky young man whom I met when I attended night school. We played chess before, during and after class. A wheeler-dealer was Herman and it was from him that I acquired my long-lasting interest in the Stock Market and Big Business.

Horst signed. "It all seems light years away when I recall it all. Do you realize," he said, "I only know the whereabouts of Gerhard at this time. The others, well, like me they could be anywhere in the world."

Jill, fiddling with a glossy photograph, realized that she, too, did not know the whereabouts of any of her schoolgirl chums. A few of the older ones were undoubtedly dead. She studied the photo that showed a large group of women ranging in age from sixty down to the youngest toddler in the front row. 'The Old Girls of the Sacred Heart Convent' and their children ran the caption. "Look, Horst," she said, pointing to the photo, "Mother is there with me and young Chris, and there's Auntie Bibbie with her three girls and little son. I've written about some of the teachers here in the back row, too," she added, turning over the pages of her family record.

"The Gym/Games mistress, mentioned before, was either too old or too large to demonstrate or participate in any of her classes. It was this teacher, though, who before school kindly gave me posture exercises to help me stand tall and feel proud of my alarming growth. Yes, she had her favourites, and it was definitely preferable to be one of her 'pets' rather than out of her favour!

"The silver-haired Biology teacher was elegantly tall and slim. All of the girls who had crushes on her professed that this teacher had never married because of a broken love affair. She was often seen gazing wistfully out of the laboratory window.

"The oldest one here is the English teacher with the piles of soft gray curls atop her head. An Old Girl, indeed, she even taught Mother and her three sisters. She was as famous for her beautiful renditions of Shakespeare as for her flapping black gown that continuously fell from her shoulders to trail onto the floor collecting dust and chalk.

"The dusky Indian lady is the old and wizened Math teacher. She was another gazer-into-space person with an unintelligible sing-song voice and invitations to her home for tea. She had a face and voice which in the Sixties and Seventies would soon dominate the West London suburbs, causing the pale-faced Englishman to become a minority group in his own homeland."

"I recognize most of the other faces," said Jill, peering closely at the picture, "but I can't give a name to all of them. Most of them belong to girls who were seniors when I started the school. At the time of the photo they were Old Girls who were successful in the world outside those grim convent doors—as teachers, nuns and mothers."

"Gracious," added Jill, surprised. "How did I miss out the friendly French teacher with whom I also shared a birthday. I remember her voice sounded as if she was speaking through a wheezy megaphone. She also told me so despairingly that my spoken French accent sounded like a Cockney Londoner.

"Everyone in this picture over twenty-five years old is wearing a hat. I guess they are all the good Old Girls who would end the meeting by going to Benediction in the convent chapel. Even Mother, hatless in the photo, would excuse herself from this service because her youngest was fretful and her husband was waiting at home for his tea."

A shadow fell across the book in Jill's lap. She looked up to see her father looming into the light. "Why, hello Father. Coincidence, but I was just telling Horst about the Old Girl meetings at the convent and how we used to wangle our way out of going to Benediction. Mother always blamed you because she had to rush home to give you your tea"

"No idea what you're talking about, Jill," he said stepping cautiously around the debris of souvenirs. "Any chance of letting me get through to my bedroom? Whatever you're doing," he added, "don't you think you'd be a lot more comfortable downstairs?"

"We've almost finished," replied Jill "At least I think so," she added as she noticed she still had a way to go and Horst also had his parallel stories to tell.

She cleared a passageway for her father, telling him that they had been through his entire family, found the triplets and his deceased sisters but missing a brother.

With a puzzled look on his face he disappeared into his bedroom and closed the door behind him.

Horst was surprised that Jill had misplaced a relative. "Well, in a family of nine, spread out too, and if you happen to be the next to the youngest, it's quite possible that two older siblings had died in infancy and there was a brother you didn't remember," she replied in defence of her father's confused silence.

"Anyway, Horst, what was going on with you during your father's absence? He was in a prisoner-of-war camp in France, wasn't he?"

"Yes, you're right." said Horst, readying himself to speak into the microphone. "During the four years Papa was a P.O.W. in France, Mama worked to support our family of four. She was employed a few blocks from our home as a housekeeper/cleaner/laundress by the French Red Cross. Mama was an experienced housekeeper, having taken what would be called today an extensive Home Economics course. The officials were kind to her and her payment was a monthly supply of food.

"After school I had a bicycle delivery job distributing packages, for which I received 2,000 DM a week. "Oh, no, no, no," he quickly added on seeing his wife's astonished look, "that is in old worthless Marks. For example, a funfair ride cost 100 DM. At weekends I would cycle to outlying farms and barter for food. What did I use? We had nothing left of our own.

"Well, after the war an acquaintance of Mama's, the owner of a haberdashery store, asked us to store about fifty large boxes in our burnt-out bedroom. The room also housed our chickens and every time we opened the door we had to be very quiet. Any unexpected noise startled the chickens and they'd fly out of the hole in the roof. We stored the boxes and covered them with a tarpaulin for protection from the chickens and the elements.

"One day I couldn't resist taking a peek. I poked a hole in the side with a screwdriver and pried open the lid. To my surprise, I extracted silken scarves, silk stockings and other valuable items of clothing that made my weekend bartering in the country for potatoes, cabbages, butter and eggs a very successful enterprise.

"In 1949 when the new money was introduced, the lady returned for her boxes. I had been clever enough to take out over the months a few items from each box, so it was not obvious what I had done. Even though she must have realized things were missing, she had no grounds for complaint as they were black market goods. Yet, when she did re-open her shop, we never went near the place and would look the other way if we met her in the street.

"With the coal and root vegetables stolen from the freight trains, the butter, eggs, milk, fruit and fresh vegetables from the silk scarves, we were able to survive Papa's absence.

"Mama did, in fact, have a very clever ruse to obtain extra food from the farmers. Whenever she had the time off from her job, she would accompany me to the outlying farms on my bartering trips, taking with her a pack of playing cards.

"The country folk were very superstitious, as indeed were many of the town people. Mama would bring out her cards from her deep shopping bag and ask if anyone wanted to have his fortune told. She had been doing this for a year or two and her fame for bringing good luck had spread from farm to farm.

"Mama would give her melodramatic spiel, always forecasting love, fame and fortune. As the farmer's wife's eyes glistened, Mama knew our bargain hunting was going to be bountiful that day."

"What an absolutely marvelous story," said Jill, reaching over to turn off the tape recorder. "That deserves an ovation," she said clapping her hands together as Horst gave a bow. "You know," said Jill excitedly, "Mother too was magical the way she conjured up meals from our meager rations. Thrift was her second name. It's still second nature to me even now to open up the packs of loose tea to shake our every last leaf." Noticing her husband about to interrupt, she said, "Well, I used to. Okay! I know we use teabags now."

"Mother even scraped every bit of margarine and butter from its greaseproof wrapping and to this day I still use stale bread to make crumbs or cubed as a hot cereal with warm milk and sugar. That was a great favourite bedtime supper for my brothers and me just before going up the wooden hill to sleep.

"To the uninitiated or to foreigners," she said pointedly, "who go to sleep in a place called Bettenhauesen with bed-shaped houses, we children climbed the stairs, chanting the words Up The Wooden Hill on each step until we reached the top."

"Didn't we Daddy?" she called to her father as he emerged from his bedroom. "You remember our bedtimes, don't you? She noticed that he was not wearing his hearing aid, so raising her voice said, "It's nothing, Father. But do ask Mother about your family. We're trying to get it straight for the record."

He stopped on the landing. "I've been thinking about what you said. Well, I had two brothers and six sisters. Jack was the oldest and Frank the one who went to South America. Which one were you missing? Oh, Jack, well he married Gladys and had no children. Now can I go back downstairs?"

Jill and Horst laughed as she thanked her father and waved him down the stairs. Horst turned on the tape. He'd remembered a titbit he wanted to add on to his recording.

CHAPTER 20

"One hundred Ludwigshafen undernourished children were to be selected to be sent to Switzerland, a neutral country during the war, as you know, as the guests of families who would return them fit and well fed. Mama told me to apply even though she needed me as her helper. However, she would be able to retain my ration card which would mean extra food for my siblings. Mama coached me for the interview. I was to speak softly, look wan and say I suffered from fainting spells. In anticipation of my trip to the alpine mountains with green meadows and cows, I packed my few belongings and was ready to depart immediately after my examination. The nurse at the Social Service office poked my thin ribs and squeezed my meager flesh. She announced that I was not thin enough to qualify. There were other children more deserving. My dreams were never fulfilled and neither did Mama get the extra rations."

As he turned off the recording, Jill put her arms around her husband, hugging the wartime boy. "What a tragedy, you poor thing. I never had it that hard. Though I did have hot ray treatment at a hospital to toughen me up after the bout of whooping cough. I remember wearing special goggles to protect our eyes as I pranced around naked with fat Junior under the warm lights. But that's when I was very little and way before the war."

"Anyhow, that's neither here nor there," she added, grinning. "While you were struggling to survive in the French occupied zone, let me now tell you a sad story concerning my experiences with the French at about the same time.

Horst was interested, wondering what adventures she was about to relate. As victors in the war and with the French as allies, the account couldn't be too horrendous.

"Promise me one thing though, lieb, will you? She spoke earnestly while trying to disguise a smile. "Don't get annoyed when you reach the end of the tale. Promise? It's really quite sad."

"I don't know what you're talking about, but, okay, I promise," he replied half-heartedly. Jill turned the page of her book and handed it to her husband. She wanted him to read it himself. He took the book with a questioning look and began to read.

"When Mother announced that we were to have yet another French visitor, I was instantly dismayed and wary. Both Peter and I had only very recently experienced disastrous exchanges with natives from across the English Channel. "Mother," we pleaded, "how could you. It's going to be awful." Had she so quickly forgotten the miseries of the two debacles?

"Both our exchange visits with a student from a French family, as arranged through our schools, had been dismal failures. Not only had there been complete incompatibility of personalities, but also our linguistic abilities had scarcely improved beyond a reflexive response of 'Oui' or 'Non" with our French accents still as non-nasal as before.

"How exciting it had been when Jacques was the selection for Peter. The accompanying photograph with vital statistics showed a handsome, dark-haired young man. He lived with his affluent parents in a chateau in the beautiful Loire Valley, which was hardly comparable to our Chiswick semi-detached home in the concrete streets of London. The similarities in selection worsened on the discovery that Jacques was an only child, and we were four, extremely shy, word-shy, people shy, world shy and with very limited English. The cardinal sin of omission was that he didn't play tennis, the absolute requisite and number one priority on Peter's application.

"So it had been a total disaster, with poor Mother left to entertain this guileless Gaul after Peter had long since departed early every morning for the courts. When timid, silent Jacques finally did return to France after a tedious three weeks for us all, he left behind, mingled with relief, a most peculiar, penetrating foreign odour in his room—a mixture of staleness and perspired un-named herbs—that lingered long after the strain of his presence had departed.

"When my turn came, Mother was determined that the selection would be the correct one, as far as was possible from a few vital statistics and a hazy photo. The choice lay between two candidates, both equally as ominous—a fourteen year old boy or a seventeen year old girl. I decided that I would undoubtedly not be happy entertaining a short French boy of my own age, so we chose the girl, Christiane.

"As Fate would have it, she turned out to be the most beautiful, slim, shapely, dark-haired, husky-voiced, mature young lady, and being French, another five years of seductive sophistication added on. On the other hand, I, an under-developed, late blossoming, extremely thin, flat, tall fourteen year old, with nary a notion of men, make-up or mature thoughts, was totally unsuited to this mademoiselle. The three weeks I spent in her family's village was painfully boring enough, as I endured her secret rendezvous with many of the village men--twenty-four year olds were ancient to me at that age—as the innocent alibi to Christiane's strict, enquiring parents. Even the dirty ditty learned during the secret soirees I was forbidden to sing during supper. A swift kick under the table shut me up!

"How I dreaded her return visit, and how Mother insisted that I be the gracious hostess! Things, however, didn't turn out quite so badly for she became the toast of the uncles. An unattached one took over my duties with relish by escorting Christiane all over London, making sure she suffered not one moment of boredom.

"So the impending arrival of another Continental, a French male, was not met with much joy. 'Well, that's how it's going to be,' uttered Mother quite light-heartedly, I thought, for such awful news. How could she! 'You might even enjoy it,' were Mother's final words to me. How right she was.

"The moment Pierre was introduced to me, it was love at first sight. With curly black hair and dancing dark eyes, he was handsome, charming, capricious, suave, and took to me instantly. We became inseparable, spending all our time together and going for endless walks over Ealing Common. He was a devoted and ardent listener, hanging onto my every word and step, never interrupting or contradicting as he gave me dog-like devotion. We were twin souls. Even in appearance I emulated his dark black locks with a curly top-knot and wavy locks around my face. I loved this Frenchie, even when he became over-excited and playfully tried to push me over to smother me with sweet, moist kisses and demands. It was all so endearing, as he was just being the typical, temperamental, lovable and super-sensitive Frenchman.

"And then came the dreadful day of the accident when he was hit by a car down the busy avenue on our of our afternoon walks on the Common. As the car screeched to a halt, I rushed to the still body lying in the road. 'Is he alright?' asked the driver, white-faced and tense as he rushed to my side. 'I didn't see him. I couldn't stop.'

"'He's just unconscious, isn't he?' I asked through my tears. Not a drop of blood or any sign of injury was to be seen. All the way to the hospital, as I held the heavy body of my dear Pierre, I lived in hope, until the grave-faced doctor said that it had been instantaneous and he had not suffered at all!

"The remorseful driver drove me home, numb and stupefied as I was. When Mother answered my frantic ringing at the doorbell and saw me sobbing and distraught, a strange man at my side, a rush of awful incidents passed through her mind. I sobbed out the dreadful news amid torrents of tears as Mother put a comforting arm around me to lead me indoors.

"She turned to the kind, guilt-ridden driver and said softly, 'Thank you so much for coming here. It wasn't your fault. There's nothing you could have done. He shouldn't have been taken off his leash so close to the road. Thank you again and goodbye.'"

Horst was silent for a moment, then yelled, "Du Spassmacher! You joker, you! You stinker!"

"I warned you, didn't I," said Jill with a laugh.

"I was torn between jealously and sorrow, and then you had to give me an ending like that," said Horst, disgusted with himself for being taken in.

"Incidentally," added Jill, "Pierre was irreplaceable. Mother quickly got a new poodle, but he was irritable and snappy with none of Pierre's charm. So that one didn't last long either. He went back to the kennels." She picked up a photo and flipped through her book, and added with a glance at her husband, "and back to the book, Horst?"

Although he wasn't about to be appeased so quickly, he reluctantly agreed. "This one's quite innocuous, don't worry, and no more tricks" she promised.

CHAPTER 21

"Here's a 2x3 snapshot of two girls in their early teens, Mary and me, holding tennis racquets and clad in sparkling white tennis outfits—Persil-white blouses, freshly whitened plimsolls, neatly folded-over ankle socks and pleated skirts reaching to just above the knee, (quite daring considering our school skirts had to reach the floor when kneeling.) But why Mary with the tennis racquet? I can't imagine. She was not a tennis player. We were friends for other things.

"Mary was the youngest, unplanned one of seven children. Her mother, the silver-haired wiry Irish nurse who supervised the laying-out of Grandma Field, one day confided in Mother's busy ear. While Mother, with little time for gossip or chat, bustled around the kitchen trying to meet the needs of a young family, Mary's mother confessed that her last child was the result of unwelcome attention from her drunken husband.

"This was my era of the 3-speed racing bicycle of eggshell blue with dropped chrome handlebars. With my friend Barbara from the convent and her younger sister, (whose feisty little cockney mother would insist join us in all our ventures) we spent our summer days dashing down the cycle path of the Great West Road to the fields and small towns of Greater London.

"That exciting Saturday in July when we three queued up for hours to get into Wimbledon's Centre Court for the Men's Singles Finals to stand in a tight crush for long, lovely hours. Under the beautiful blue sky we cheered on Macgregor, the American refrigerator salesman, facing across the net his rival for the cup, the little Czech, Drobny. The first set was magnificent. Each player won his serve with nonstop aces. The set climaxed in a heart-stopping exhausting 34-32 to Macgregor!

"We were also a great tennis team. We were either off to play at a local club or off on a bike-ride. Speeding off on our bikes, we'd turn and wave to my friends' mother, sending us off from the top window of their tiny two roomed Council flat. There she tended her hairdressing business as well as her little gnome-like, gray-haired, Czech immigrant husband, (no wonder my friends were despondent when Drobny lost), with little English and a tendency to sit endlessly by the fireside.

"However, it was with Mary that I found the intimacy of close peers, separate from our school friendships. Many an hour I spent in her rambling house on the corner of our Chiswick road as we both kept out of the way of her huge, morose father. I enjoyed being among her numerous grownup siblings and away from the noise and demands of my own younger, clinging brothers and cousins.

"It was with Mary that I went to church every Sunday. Sometimes we walked to the sung mass where I'd see Auntie May warbling away in the choir. Other times we attended the noon service with its long sermon. How frighteningly exciting it was to hear the statuesque priest shout from the pulpit at anyone who was late arriving. 'You're late,' he'd shout in his stentorian voice to the unfortunate parishioner hovering in the doorway. 'Next time the door will be closed in your face!'

"Father always insisted that we children attend Mass every Sunday. We had to be at death's door to miss church. Even one time when I pleaded illness, I had to go. How I relished rushing back home to tell him that I'd been sick all over the pew and had to be escorted outside into the fresh air!

"It was with Mary that I spent hours in the library selecting the latest adventure stories for girls. Although Enid Blyton was a favourite when I was younger, I then favoured the Worrals adventures of a female wartime protagonist, as did Peter avidly read about Biggles, her male counterpart. Mother often asked me to go to the adult section to get a book for her. I had to ask the librarian for a 'deep' book, and felt foolish when unable to explain what I meant. How relieved I was when the book she handed me was one Mother relished reading."

Jill turned to Horst. "That reminds me. When we first lived in Germany in that village, the library there was small and old-fashioned. We weren't allowed to go to the shelves to select a book but had to ask at the counter either for a specific title or the type of reading we wanted. Since there were only very few books in English, the librarian got fed up bringing out each book which I rejected as having read. Finally, when I learned the German word for 'deep' and insisted on such a book, she allowed me into the inner sanctum to look for myself and browse at leisure." Horst laughed. He'd never heard that before. Jill continued reading about Mary.

"It was with Mary that I went down to the River Thames to watch the annual Boat Race pass by. Standing on a cold march day on the muddy bank, I cheered for Cambridge University, the light blues, while Mary egged on Oxford, the dark blues.

"It was with Mary that I went to our weekly Girl Guide meetings in a local school hall. All I ever seemed to learn were intricate knots demonstrated by the older girls into a twisting pathway of sexually insinuating ropes, weaving up, in, through and around the curving loops. I returned home those evenings after a long walk along the lighted High Road into the bright lights of our kitchen. There I'd find mother and Father with the Moores, Lollie and Spence, in their customary enjoyment of arguments and tears among the Bridge cards!

"But it was with Jennifer that I spent a three week holiday in Norway. Neither Mary nor Barbara's parents could afford the fare, so Mother encouraged me to ask Jennifer, a school friend. Her parents were more affluent with a corner haberdashery shop in the heart of seedy Shepherd's Bush. Jennifer was also the daughter of an Old Girl who had been at the convent school with Mother and her sisters.

"In his teens Peter had developed into a clever young man. Along with another boy, he was chosen by our local Member of Parliament, Francis Noel-Baker, to represent our borough in an Oslo home as true, upright British boyhood. The trip was a great success. Hans, the older son, was a keen tennis player (how he awed us as he played barefoot on the hard tarmac court) and a very satisfactory partner for Peter. Following their exchanges, it was my turn to be invited along with a friend.

"We had a marvelous time despite the train journey to Hull to board the ship. I lost my ticket on the way and was unable to produce it for the inspector. After a lot of hargy-bargy, I was finally allowed onto the cruise ship for the day's trip across the North Sea to Norway. This was our first taste of elegant living and sophisticated socializing. We were two thirteen year olds on our first trip out of the country. Traveling first class we were unsure how to conduct ourselves, especially regarding the huge lobster that sat regally pink with black beady eyes and pinched claws among other delicacies on the groaning table. So we spent the time sitting quietly and silently conducting ourselves like the good, young Convent girls that we were!

"It must have been this holiday that opened my eyes to the marvels of the male sex around us. I'd never considered my brothers as men, let alone belonging to mankind. Displayed before us during the entire vacation were some of the most handsome, tall, gorgeous, charming, blonde creatures ever to be seen. How upset I was when I twisted my foot in an unseen hole during an especially rough game of croquet. Just as I was getting the hang of dancing, fishing and swimming with these young men, I had to spend the rest of the time with a sprained ankle alone in a hammock. Jennifer cavorted off with the rest of the young people to the various parts of the delightful holiday island of Vasser, the summer home of the Norwegian doctor and his family.

"On our return home Jennifer and I remained good friends. It became quite a Sunday routine to meet up at the Abbey attached to our brothers' school. There we would sit as close as possible to the all-male school choir and ogle the cassocked pupils throughout the service.

"Mike and Christopher didn't attend ordinary schools as had Peter and I during the war years of little money. Mother and Father were able to afford the private boys' school run by the Benedictine monks. About two miles from our home, it was attached to the magnificent Abbey with its Norman architecture and stained-glass windows. Peter forever regretted that he didn't have the advantaged education of his younger brothers. Yet, he would in the long run make the greatest achievements of us all, despite being the only one of his upper-class socialite friends who had not been nurtured along the social paths of private schools—or used that springboard to higher education at a university.

"Mike was unsuited to the school, for not only being non-academic, he also held pacifist views. Once when refusing to don the army uniform of the school Corp and after a thrashing from the sadistic Corp brother, he ran away from home rather than face Father's anger when the sergeant major's report arrived in the post. Mike artfully asked for a few pounds from the then manageress of the wine shop and took a train to the country cousins' home. He spent the night in the field behind their house, next to the long-gone bull, not daring to face Auntie Evie's strict husband either.

"The police were unperturbed. They knew he would turn up when hungry. However, poor Mother and Father had to endure a night of anguish before the recalcitrant youth, bedraggled, cold and hungry, dared to venture in from the cornfield.

"I wonder if Mike remembers his six weeks evacuation there many, many years ago when he was the chosen child?

"Quite boy-oriented I was becoming. I remember the admiring comments and looks I received from my fellow Sixth Formers when I made a special request to the headmistress, a nun renowned for her strictness and long pointed nose which preceded the arrival of her wimple by at least an inch. I bravely asked if we could have the Sixth Form boys from the Abbey school over for a Christmas dance. She was very understanding and appeared quite amused. However, it couldn't possible be allowed—nor for another ten years, I believe! (When the convent eventually introduced modern ideas, they even placed a coca cola machine in those hallowed cloisters!)

"Attached to the monastery was a youth club which both Jennifer and I attended regularly. It was a hot bed for all the senior pupils of the Abbey. We watched many a romance unfold between young persons of our own age, many of which developed into serious commitments and marriages that endure to this day. Just like Father and Mother!

"That wasn't for me, however, even though I often envied the smooth-running relationships of those loving couples. I found it all rather boring! A few years later when my best friend at work became engaged at age eighteen and immediately started to save sixpences in a jar for her far-off wedding, I decided it was absolutely dreadful to be in such a rut at such an early age.

"Goodness gracious, there was a whole wonderful world waiting out there for me!"

Jill closed the book and thought of the years that had transpired since that time. Their own children were even on the thresholds of their own lives.

Her dreaming and Horst's cough to get her attention to start his next story about his holiday after the war was interrupted by Mother calling from the stairs.

"You've got us all going on the family tree. Daddy's sorted out his family of nine, he says, and his mother with the triplets. And mine has the seven with the three boys and four girls, myself and your three aunts." Jill called out her thanks, relieved that the maze had sorted itself out and that triplets had skipped her generation.

"Such a complicated family you have," sighed Horst. "Mine is all so straightforward. How I wish I'd followed up on the rumour about a great grandfather from Poland who was hanged as a robber. What do you think of that?"

"Sounds interesting, but you'll have to do lots of research, or at least talk to your parents. Until then, get on with your next story."

CHAPTER 22

"I also started venturing out into the world," said Horst, "though not in such luxury as you, Jill."

"I was fourteen years old during the summer vacation of 1947, which in those days was from June to September, and now is not so long and staggered from area to area over eight weeks. It was decided to send me to Bavaria in southern Germany to work on a farm in return for flour and butter which I would bring back to Ludwigshafen.

"I went to the freight train station, there being no passenger trains, and waited with crowds of people for a train going in the direction of Munich. The only way to know was by asking the engine driver which way he was headed.

"I found a train and hopped on, sitting precariously on the edge of an open wagon which was doorless and roofless. It took me three days to get to Landshut, a town about twenty miles from the farm. A horse and cart loaded with metal milk containers was headed towards Tattendorf, my destination. The driver told me I could join him. We clanked our way through villages and hamlets and countryside where Time seemed to have stood still. The old weather-beaten, leathery-faced driver was only just aware that there had recently been a World War!

"I arrived at the farm and was met by the owner, a caricature of a Bavarian, wearing an old green feathered hat on top of a wrinkled face with an immense bristling moustache. He wore an embroidered bolero, three quarter-length leather trousers, tight thick long socks just-below-the-knee and shoes that looked as if they had been worn by many previous generations.

"The farmer had three sons of whom he'd had no news since leaving for the Russian Front. He also had four daughters, aged fifteen to twenty-one, all lusty, solidly-built with shiny round healthy-looking faces and arms like weight-lifters.

"Oma was still there with her daughter-in-law and her two children, my cousins. The older one would many years later die of pneumonia in divided Berlin. My uncle, Oma's favourite child, was presumed dead at the Russian Front.

"My task was to clean out the cow stables with its twenty cows, the pig pens with its 15 pigs and take out the cows to a distant meadow, then bring them home again in the late afternoon.

"Hans, a neighbouring farmer's son, trained me. The meadows were bordered on three sides with the fourth one open. The cows were driven to the end of the meadow and I, the cowherd, would return to the open side and slowly await the munching cows make their way through the grass. When they finally arrived at the unguarded opening, my job was to drive them back again and go through the whole procedure again. It was a tedious and toilsome job. However, Hans taught me the 'mosquito' trick which was to make a ZZZZ noise like a mosquito. On hearing the sound, the cows would prick up their ears, turn around, and, believe it or not, with tails raised high in the air, race back to the other side of the meadow to again slowly resume their wandering way back across the field. This ruse allowed me to lie in the grass and gaze up into the sun-filled sky.

"While I cleaned the stables the girls milked the cows and filled the troughs. Since they never had any contact with the outside world, they would beg me to sing and whistle all the latest German and American hit songs. As the only 'foreign' male around, I was very much appreciated. Frequently they would invite me into their bedroom where all four slept in one room. I was invited to move from bed to bed, cuddling and kissing as I told them stories of the big wide world!

"Mealtimes were a very special occasion. All the old farmhands, daughters, the farmer, his wife, me, Oma, my aunt and my cousins, would sit around a huge round oaken table in the center of which stood a three-foot wide bowl brim full of delicious smelling steaming gruel, soup or stew. After saying Grace, the words of which I never fully understood, being a Protestant in a Catholic area, everyone pulled out a spoon and knife from the pocket of their leather pants or skirt and proceeded to dip into the central bowl. Since there were no plates, at the end of the meal there was a dribbling line of food from the bowl to each person's place.

"A two gallon stein of beer was passed continuously around the table. The old farmer made sure that his moustache received a good wash every time he took a sip. At the end of the meal the stein had an inch of sediment on the bottom. I dared not, however, ever clean off the brim as it was passed to me for a swig.

"Most of the wagons were pulled by oxen. Two horses were reserved for Sundays and they would pull a long coach full of all of us going to church. The farmer and his wife would ask forgiveness for having killed a pig during the week, which together with 50 lbs of butter, they had supplied to the Black Market.

"Four months later and with fifty pounds of flour and twenty pounds of butter as payment for my work, I made my way home. I said goodbye to my hardworking Oma whom I would not see for another seven years until I came to the rescue of my uncle who had bought a bakery on his return from the Russian Front.

"It was back to school then. Summer was over. The next year was uneventful until finally the great day arrived. Papa was being released from the prisoner-of-war camp. We were given one day's notice.

"As I walked into the downstairs entrance hall of our apartment building, one of my friends called out, 'Horst, your father's home!'

"Ha, ha! I don't believe you!"

"'Yes he is. I saw him arrive!' I flew up the eight flights of stairs two at a time. As I unlatched the front door I heard Papa's voice in the kitchen. There he sat at the kitchen table, thin, gaunt and haggard. He had spent the past three years as a prisoner after his arrest by the occupying American forces on their entry into Germany at the end of the war.

"At that time he was led outside the police station with his fellow police officers, disarmed and forced to lie face down on the cobbled street for several hours. Papa remembers hearing one big, black American sergeant shouting, 'Everyone is to lie completely still. No-one is to move, not even to piss.' When they were all finally allowed to get up and led to the awaiting trucks for transport to France, it is not difficult to image the unpleasant stench lingering long after the departure of Papa and his compatriots.

"Up until the end of the war, Papa later told me, they were well treated and given sufficient food. But then in 1945 at war's end when all Allied prisoners had been repatriated and there could be no more reprisal for bad treatment towards them, the daily ration was cut to a bare minimum. Their main diet was composed of cornflakes and milk three times a day, a diet that incidentally cured Papa's life-long stomach ulcer for ever. His worries were minimal too, for the threat of death was removed, and he knew from our Red Cross letters that his family was surviving during the difficult post-war period.

"Seated around the kitchen table on the day of his return, Mama asked him 'Are you hungry? I've got something very special. Something we don't see very often.' She went to the larder and brought out a stick of butter which she blithely tossed into the air and cleverly caught. Papa said, 'What, butter?' to which Mama proudly replied 'Yes'. I was deeply hurt that she hadn't mentioned that I had obtained the precious substance on my previous weekend's bartering trip.

"Bread was brought out, sliced and the butter spread onto it. I was so happy to see Papa again, yet embarrassed before this sad, silent, morose man. In my anxiety to appear unabashed, I accidentally knocked over a jug of liquid. Whatever it was, I don't remember, but it soiled the table cloth.

"Papa rose out of his silence and reacted with a stinging slap to my face. I couldn't believe it! 'From now on order and discipline will rule again in this house,' he shouted.

"Stunned and deeply hurt, for Mama did not rise to my defence, I know now that in spite of having been the man of the house for so long, Papa was not about to believe that a sixteen year old could ever have taken over his duties satisfactorily.

"I was dethroned. The husband and wife team took over and I was sent back to my position as son where I belonged.

"It would be many years before I was mature enough to accept what had happened and to become close to my father again."

Jill was amazed, yet pleased, to hear her husband's confession. Maybe the time was ripe to expose her own jealous scene. She leafed through the book.

On finding the page, she said to Horst, 'Well, thanks for sharing that with me, liebling. It might be an appropriate time to read you the doll episode I mentioned earlier.' Horst agreed, but first he wanted to finish up with his father's story. He continued:-

"Papa had to be denazified on his return from the prisoner-of-war camp. Until that happened he worked as a labourer in a junk yard in Ludwigshafen, anything that would bring in some money for the family. Although a demeaning job, he later admitted to me that it was one of the happiest times of his life. The simple outdoor life appealed to him, as compared to later years when he was reinstated to the lower ranks of the police force. It took him a further seventeen years to reach his previous rank of major.

"Denazification was for Papa a comparatively simple affair for he was on one of the lower rungs of the Nazi Party ladder, in fact very low in the hierarchy. At the Nuremburg Trials conducted after the war for Nazi crimes, many paid the supreme penalty of death. In Papa's case he was called to the Town Council where he was reprimanded by the new German Government officials. He had to swear to be a law-abiding democratic citizen and to pay a fine of 100 DM.

"Opa Schaefer, who was held in high esteem by the new Social Democratic Government and brought out of retirement to teach during the war, wrote a letter confirming his son's allegiance to democratic principles."

After that interesting slice of history, Jill thought her own story rather petty. "But you made such a mystery about it, Jill, and I want to hear it" he insisted.

"Well, alright then," she agreed reluctantly. "This is the other doll episode I mentioned earlier," she said, pointing to an 8x10 black and white flashlight photo taken in a nightclub, or restaurant, as there were waiters hovering in the background. She turned to the book and read:-

"Four adults dressed in evening dress at a formal occasion. Auntie Lollie, smiling and elegant with fingers waves of gold, a corsage pinned on her deep V-necked gown, a sparkling necklace adorning her neck. Uncle Spence, tanned and handsome with his dark crinkly hair is smartly-suited and seated at her side around a table set for dining. This must have been during their affluence days in Osterley on the outskirts of London, close to my biking days on the Great West Road. They had moved from their upstairs home in our Chiswick road to their own house, complete with French au pair girl, or Mother's help, for their small son and daughter. Father's Help was she as well, for she gave private lessons to Uncle to improve his conversational abilities for the family's many vacations spent on the French Riviera.

"The couple seated to their right is Mother and Father, looking somewhat startled, possibly from the flash, but were obviously enjoying themselves. But were they? Could they? For I remember I had most likely ruined that evening for them. That was the night Father asked me to admire that other beautiful doll!"

Horst kept quiet while stealing a quick glance at his wife's intense face, and thought, 'Confessions of a secret diary coming up, I suspect. This must be soul-bearing time for us both.' He listened to her words.

"Doesn't your mother look lovely tonight?" asked Father, slim and elegant in his black-tie suit, gushingly, of me, a lanky, nondescript fourteen-year old already taller than him. He stood at the bottom of the maroon carpeted stairs as he lovingly watched Mother's slow, regal descent for yet another social evening out. I was caught there accidentally and off guard, hoping to pass through the hallway unnoticed on my way to the kitchen from my bedroom.

"I knew his question was rhetorical and that nothing more than mumbled appreciation and due homage were expected. Much as I hated to admit, Mother did indeed look stunning as she slowly wended her way down each stair. I watched her carefully glancing down and deftly adjusting the long sweeping hem of her well-fitting deep décolleté gown of jade green satin that enhanced her womanly curves and blond bobbed curls

"Would I, could I, ever look like that? the sweet young girl in me wondered. 'You won't, and don't ever want to either,' retorted the other rebellious, jealous young woman.

"So I gave him an answer. 'Yes, she does—like a cheap tart!' As I spat out the wounding words, I watched with joy and sorrow as they hit their mark. Father's face, suffused dark red with sudden anger, barked out, 'Apologize to your mother immediately.' Mother, stopped short on the stairs, looked down in anguish at me and said sadly, 'Oh, how could you!'

"I turned and ran from them upset and hating everyone and myself. I had done a good job of spoiling their evening as well as my own!"

Jill grimaced as she lay down the book. Horst empathized with her, knowing full well how such memories hurt. But Jill, quickly recovered, had noticed another expose. "Do you have the patience to hear another?" This time it's with Peter and," she added mysteriously, 'it's a watery one, too." That made Horst very curious and also started him remembering some of his own watery adventures.

"Let me tell mine first," he pleaded. "It's a good one and I don't want to forget it." Jill closed her book and allowed him to go ahead.

CHAPTER 23

"In 1948 the River Rhein was pure, clean and full of fish in its swiftly flowing current. It was the playground of the young. Today it is polluted, the fish are gone and there are signs up saying 'No swimming allowed'" said Horst. "I'll tell you of my adventures there.

"The distance from the Mannheim bank of the river to the Ludwigshafen side is about 350 yards. I had a girl friend who was a very strong swimmer and together we would swim across to a small bird sanctuary island where we would sunbathe in the nude. Our fear was not of discovery but whether or not we would return safely through the swirling Rheingold whirlpools—where, according to the fairy-tales, was hidden the Niebelungen gold. We weren't naïve enough to attempt to discover it, even if there was any truth to the story. Besides no-one had ever come back to tell!

"To enjoy the river to its utmost, it was best to swim or float back with the fierce current, which meant a mile walk upstream to commence the ride down. Often a large group of fifty boys and girls made this trip en masse, a daily event during the long, hot summer vacations.

"Tiring of the constant walk upstream, we often hitched a ride on the huge 100 foot barges, clinging onto the lifeboats being pulled behind them. The Rhein, being the transportation route from Holland to Switzerland, was a busy scene of barges loaded with bulk goods such as coal and wheat. Hanging onto the back of these barges and being pulled against the current, often the girls would lose their bras! Accidents and near misses were a daily occurrence and even the occasional fatality.

"The river bed was gravel which accentuated every sound just below the water level as we were being dragged along. Voices became clearer and the chug, chug of the boats loud and gurgling. One day we heard mingled in with these familiar noises, a loud continuous agonizing scream. One of our friends had been caught in the propeller of the barge, pulled under by the current and the opposing drag of the barge, and drowned. Did this stop me? No. I was invincible!

"It was a test of nerves every time we swam in the river with accurate timing to avoid the oncoming boats as we swept back down with the swift, treacherous current. Great respect was shown to anyone who had the courage, and the energy, to make an immediate second trip clinging onto a barge upstream, having just survived the hazardous return journey.

"The large flat barges were the homes of many river families who spent their entire lives gliding up and down the Rhein from Holland in the north to Switzerland in the south where the river commenced, stopping on the way to unload or take on fresh cargo. The barges were their private floating castles and they did not take too kindly to the intrusion of wet, troublesome, thrill-seeking youths. To discourage us from clinging on for our ride upstream, they would stomp around the low-lying edge of the barge with its heavy cargo as if to stamp on our clinging fingers with their heavy shoes. This failing, they resorted to throwing vegetables at us."

"Goodness gracious," exclaimed Jill with a gasp. "What dare-devils you were! And that awful drowning didn't stop you at all. Bet your parents didn't know!"

"Mama knew," he replied. "And she was very worried." On that note, he picked up the little snapshot of a small bedraggled, waif-like creature with long match-stick legs. "So, what's your story about?"

"Father had caught, posed and snapped me for posterity," explained Jill. "Listen to my account and you'll understand."

"It was hot and humid the day I came home from the baths like a drowned rat, and in my confused state of anger and disappointment, was ready to spill the beans. But Father, crouched and concentrating on a difficult piece of crazy-paving puzzle in the back garden, was oblivious to the distress in my voice and the tears beneath my wetness. He was ready for a cigarette, a stretch and a tryout of his new camera before resuming his puzzle. He took my photo, then noticing my dampness told me to dry off and change my clothes—and that Mother was still at the park with Junior and Christopher. So, it wasn't until an hour later at supper that anything came out about what had happened that afternoon.

"Summers in our west London suburb were especially fortunate for we boasted the only outdoor swimming pool in the area, or rather, two pools end to end. The old bath was gray and sunless. The new popular one was brilliantly blue-tiled and in a good sunny position. It was surrounded by an expansive lawn with its lush green grass hidden beneath a patchwork of towels. Some staked out territory while others were adorned by silent sun-worshippers and happy families, picnicking, relaxing and sunning.

"The deep end was for the accomplished swimmers and the high divers who enjoyed showing off their expertise to the cheers and applause of the appreciative sun packed crowd; the bathing belles who wanted to be picked and chatted up and thrown in screaming with frenzied delight; and the gangs of teenage toughs just waiting to push into the deep water any unsuspecting timid fool hovering on the edge or any likely-looking victim harmlessly walking by. The azure water of the shallow end was scarcely visible among the screams and squirms of splashing non-swimmers and the daring ones who jumped from the sides into the over-chlorinated water to pop up quickly like playful porpoises.

"Still a non-swimmer at age twelve, I preferred to brave the coolness of the old shallow pool. There with my friends Mary and Pam, we could enjoy relative privacy in our attempts to swim without the many interruptions of a breathless, indignant body doing its assigned number of widths, or when we jumped off the side, the chance meeting of a headless kicking torso. Our favourite game was Ring a ring of Roses, when at All Fall Down, we ducked under with noses held and eyes open to oversee each other while silently counting to see who could stay under the longest without coming for air!" She glanced up.

"Phew," she said, catching her breath. "That was quite a rambling sentence to read without stopping for air." Horst groaned and waved her on.

"However." she continued, "that day Mary and I had gone to the baths alone. I hadn't invited Pam because just the previous week she had suddenly found herself able to swim. How she'd bored me to tears when, chilled and hungry, I was ready to go home. Delighting in her new expertise, she refused to leave the water and kept swimming on and on. So Mary, still in my league, was my choice of companion that day.

"It was always an interesting mile walk to the baths in the sunshine. Past the 'rec' playground, the allotments, and across the roundabout to a short-cut through the deserted wharves lining the River Thames, through the cemetery and onto the baths. On the way, fifteen year old Peter and his friends on bicycles passed us and teased us with threats of 'teaching us how to swim' if they saw us at the baths. When we finally arrived, we joined the long, fast-moving shuffle of dry, dusty people, all eager to pay up and glance up at the chalked-up temperature of 68 degrees (or 72, if we were lucky). We were fortunate to find an empty changing room, so didn't have to expose our presence to Peter by asking to use his.

"Mary and I spent the afternoon doing our usual sunless antics although it wasn't quite as much fun with just the two of us. So at long last we decided to warm up in the sun of the new pool, watch the divers from the side and then get dressed and walk home. We made our way through the center building which housed the turnstiles, pay booths and showers. On the roof was a patio where the beef-cake boys and brown bikinied girls showed off with breathtaking acrobatics and languid poses.

As I cautiously trod through the slippery puddles and avoided the bullying boys around the deep end, suddenly a forceful push flung me over the side. I landed with a painful smack in the deep water which immediately closed over my head. I went down and came up quickly. Relieved that it was all over so painlessly, I groped for and failed to grab the side. As I looked up and around for a helping hand, I noticed Peter, who appeared to be gazing down at me with a sardonic grin on his face, as if to say 'Come on now, little sister, show us how you can swim.'

"Helplessly I sunk below the surface again. I flailed and flapped my limbs as the blue-white water surged up bubbling past my open eyes. With nose tingling, ears roaring, and chest beginning to suffocate, I momentarily poised on the bottom, then with bursting lungs glided up towards the surface to break air.

Gasping, I again reached for and failed to grab the side. As I clawed at the water around my partially submerged face, I gurgled out to Peter, now standing stock still and staring stonily as if transfixed, and with frantic eyes and faint watery gasps signaled desperately to him, to anybody. 'Help me. Somebody, please help me. I can't swim!' I knew if I went down again, I'd never come up.

"Helpless against the magnetic force as it swiftly drew me under for the final time, away from the breath and hub-bub of life above, the blanket of water closed over my mouth, nose, head, arms and finally finger-tips, to sink slowly into the deep watery tomb. I floated unresistingly down to a watery grave, no more choking or struggling against the ascending bursts of bubbles streaming past me in the serenity of my final silent descent. 'Why didn't Peter help me? I'll tell Mummy and Daddy when I get home,' I told myself dreamily.

"Suddenly a firm, strong grip under my elbow and another around my waist, propelled me up to burst swiftly to the surface. Gasping and choking, I was helped by my unknown rescuer to the side where I lay like a beached whale.

All appeared as normal. Swimmers stood or ran by above my head. The noise was stupendous and alive with laughter and shouts. Shocked and trembling, I gulped the delicious air and looked up among all the feet into the throng of faces and into Peter's eyes. He was still standing there. He hadn't moved at all. He gave me one look of relief and disappeared into the crowd.

"As if to comfort me on our weary way home, Mary said, "I'm sure Peter didn't push you in."

"But he didn't try to save me either," was my confused and sad reply. "I could have drowned for all he cared."

As I was listening to the 5 o'clock Children's Hour on the wireless, feeling a little calmer and anger somewhat abated, Peter came into the room and looked at me rather sheepishly. 'Look,' he said, 'you're okay, aren't you? I was just about to dive in and haul you out when that man beat me to it. You know I wouldn't have let you drown, don't you, you silly-billy.' Although I knew he feared getting into trouble if I told our parents, he was also trying to apologize for having let us both down that day.

"Did you enjoy yourselves at the baths today," came the rhetorical question during the family meal.

"Yes, until somebody pushed me in the deep end. I went under three times and almost drowned." Heads raised, knives and forks poised as I poured out my tale of woe, ending with 'But someone saved me at the last moment!' Wondering whether to be alarmed or proud at the identity of the someone, Mother and Father stared at my pale-faced brother with consternation, wondering if he had anything to do with it. 'No,' I said quickly. 'It wasn't him. He didn't push me in. He was going to save me but somebody else got there first. Peter wouldn't have let me drown.' I received a lot of comfort and Peter got a telling off for not looking after his sister. It could have been worse for both of us.

"Hmm," said Horst, wondering how often he and his own sister had clashed in their youth. "So that's why you're never keen to put your head under water. Your story explains everything."

"I suppose so," said Jill. "I can tell you though, I soon learned how to swim after that experience!"

"Well, we've both shared our watery experiences. What next? asked Horst, eager to tell of his post war life in war-torn Germany.

"Well, I could jump ahead some years to where I really go out into the world. Not a mere 12 feet of water, but the long distance to the center of London, all of ten miles, where I got my first job on leaving school," replied Jill. "Unless you're good and ready."

CHAPTER 24

"In 1950," said Horst, "the family council decided that butchers and bakers had come through best of all during the hard times of the war. To guard against any future misfortune and to help feed the family, I commenced an apprenticeship of three years in a local bakery. My teacher, the master baker, was an old tyrant who worked me from 4 a.m. until afternoon, ten hours of daily slavery. I received a meager wage and an abundance of bread.

"His idea of entertainment for his employees was to put a mouse into the hot oven and make us watch its legs become shorter and shorter as it scampered around in agony. It would then explode and I would have to clean out the resulting mess!

"Also, one day as I was taking a hot crusty loaf of bread out of the oven, it fell off the board onto my arm and gashed it. This sadistic boss advised me to rub salt into the wound to heal it. I did as he said, but, of course, it stung horribly and I screamed with pain. He laughed his head off as I rushed to wash out the salt. The wound remained open, red and sore for a long time as it slowly healed. I still have the scar to this day."

Horst rolled up the sleeve of his right arm to show Jill the deep two inch long scar. "Ooh," she said, wincing. "That's dreadful. What else did this monster do?"

"Nothing quite as bad as the mouse or the salt," he replied. "He got quite a kick, though, out of artfully throwing flour on the back of any unsuspecting salesman who left the bakery with his black business suit dusted with flour. I thought this very funny and often tried it myself!

"After two and a half years of hard slog, I completed my apprenticeship and became a qualified baker. I decided it wasn't the kind of work I wanted to do so applied for and was accepted as an apprentice in a commercial and technical company. There I spent three months working in all the departments, including shipping, bookkeeping, machine parts design and working in the factory. I completed this apprenticeship in 1945 and moved on to various other local companies until 1959 when I decided to become an Interpreter in English and sought to perfect my skills.

"During these years I was burning the candle at both ends and, partly from being a natural worrier like Papa, I developed stomach troubles. Doubled up with pain after a glass of wine, an ulcer was diagnosed. In 1955 the ulcer perforated and I was rushed into hospital, having lost a lot of blood. The doctors decided to cut out two thirds of my stomach, but Papa, experienced with stomach disorders, decided against it. He believed the problem would erupt elsewhere. He was quite right, for without the operation, I learned over the years to control my nervous tension and adapt my diet. The ulcer disappeared from view."

Surprised, Jill said, "You're right, Horst. You do seem to have won that battle ever since the only two occurrences, one on our wedding night, and other shortly after we'd moved to Germany."

"Well," he said proudly, "take charge of your own life, and you can't go wrong," and added with a smile, "although I certainly wasn't laughing then. And neither was I, thought Jill, grimacing, as she remembered his long six weeks in hospital, and she a new bride in a strange land. Horst pointed to her book. "And what were you doing while I was being tortured and dying?" Jill began to read.

"At long last the time had come for me to leave school at age 16, having done double duty the last two years of biding my time. With so many years of schooling behind me, I wouldn't even consider my headmistress's suggestion that I go on to Digby Stuart teachers training college. Me. a teacher? Oh no! There was surely more to life than being a teacher, a nun or even a housewife. Anyhow, I didn't relish the thought of handing out discipline to disorderly bratty students such as we had been, or be on the receiving end of the hard time we gave the teacher trainees and young, timid nuns. Whenever we purposely created a disturbance, they never failed to dissolve in tears. Anyhow, I didn't feel I had any wisdom to impart or any desire to nurture young minds. My child-minding days were over, hopefully!

"The Old Girl network went into operation. The bank manager husband of one of Mother's 'old girl' friends gave us the inside information that the Bank of England, affectionately known as the Old Lady of Threadneedle Street, was embarking on a first-ever secretarial training course. Ten girls would be selected, five in their early twenties already in their employ and five of London's current high school graduates.

"I applied, was interviewed and accepted! I'm sure it was my proud reference to being a House Captain—the type of girl dedicated to duty, diligence and discipline—that swung it. What a coup! Not only was I free of school, but would also obtain a year's highly desirable, completely free, first-class clerical training from the auspicious Bank of England—who would also pay me, a mere pittance to be sure, and then give me a job within the Bank's vast bosom.

"Regrettable though it was, this was the one and only secretarial course the Bank undertook . What possible reason could they have to repeat the entire process on an annual basis? Their moulded, meticulously trained girls grabbed their diplomas and headed for better paid, exciting positions in the City of London. As for myself, I endured the course, school-like as it was in its discipline and scholarly atmosphere, graduated with honours and placed in the shorthand-typing pool of the vast Accounting Office. How pleasant it was finally to work among businessmen after the confining year of nothing but women!

"The financial section of London, the City, was where the imposing, old buildings of the Bank of England, the Lord Mayor's Mansion House and the famous Guildhall were situated. It was an adventurous, learning experience whenever I ventured past the pink frock-coated Bank messengers and out of those huge, impressive doors of the Bank. I traveled daily from the suburbs by underground, passing bomb sites, many of which were still derelict and overgrown or dotted with flimsy, long-time temporary prefabricated houses. The skyline of London was changing with its modern high-rise matchbox buildings, incongruously set among and dwarfing magnificent period pieces of architecture which had miraculously escaped the bombs of the six and a half long years of war. Upon leaving the underground, I rose up out of the ground at Bank station into a world of centuries of English history.

"To reach the Bank of England's lunch room a short walk away, we young school-leavers embarked on a historical tour of sixteenth century London. Along narrow cobbled streets, enclosed on either side by terraces of gabled house, we would go. Emerging from mean alleyways, we arrived at and passed by the high columnar Monument with its magnificent view over London. This was the site of the beginning of the Great Fire of London which while devastating the whole of London Town, incidentally stopped the spread of the dreadful Plague.

"We then arrived at Ye Olde Tavern and go down through the smoke-filled bar where the City men of dark-suited, bowler-hatted and rolled umbrella fame, were doing their deals over a quick sandwich and mug of foamy warm beer. In our lady-like basement lunch room, we ate heartily as guests of the Bank. Then it was a last-minute rush to spend the last precious forty minutes of the lunch hour listening to the latest Johnny Ray, Les Paul and Mary Ford or Frankie Laine hit song in the modern record shop. Sometimes we window-shopped or tried on the latest fashion in the new boutiques springing up, or dashed to the street markets to pick up a bargain.

"I was seldom home for I had little spare time after work and my social activities. I ice-skated with the Bank social club, went to an evening class or stayed on in town after work. That was usually on pay-day when a friend and I grabbed a quick snack before taking in the latest Hollywood movie at one of the imposing Leicester Square cinemas.

"Television had arrived and Mother and Father were the first members of the family to get a set. In the early Fifties a favourite to watch was the memorable war programme 'Victory at Sea' with its stirring theme music. Strange how we had all so recently lived through the actual experience (we still had rationing and servicemen in our midst) that we needed to re-live it all so soon!" She paused to glance at an old newspaper Horst had in his hands. "Well, well, you know what that is, don't you? 'The King is dead,' shouted out the awful headline of the 1952 London newspaper.

"It was a gray, overcast freezing winter's day when the entire English nation, already shocked and saddened by King George VI's sudden illness, heard the dreaded-yet-expected announcement that he had gone" read Jill from her book.

"We ten young ladies studying our stenographic skills received the somber news from the thin lips of the dreaded teacher of our next clerical class. Notorious for her drill and discipline of her students, this tall, upright woman with dark hair severely drawn back into a tight bun, had the classic beauty of an Old Master's Madonna. (In fact, she was an older version of little Gonda Merlwyn of my dancing-for-the-troops days.) She quietly told us of the King's death. We were sitting in the tiny school room overlooking the roofs of old London. It was there that we had diligently learned our shorthand and typing under the auspices of our little slip of a 4'6" teacher, Miss Grailey, who deplored that we would ever graduate from her class. How we'd giggled when mis-typing an 'f' for a 'd' during the fast-paced musical typing exercise, and choked with laughter at the new version of 'The lizards are darting all over the place.' On that cold winter's day, though, we gasped and choked over our tears.

"I remember the long cold wait in the silent line of slow shuffling feet as we steadily approached to gaze sadly at the draped catafalque and with shy admiration at the stiff, silent uniformed soldiers with bowed heads who stood on guard at each corner of the raised dais. We paused momentarily to stand suitably solemn in the awe-inspiring silence as tears of sorrow sprung to our eyes--to pass on from the lying-in-state of our departed monarch out into the half-light of a bitterly cold London winter.

"He, soft-spoken and shy had taken on his popular abdicated brother's throne and duties and won over the hearts of his people. He, whose Christmas Day broadcasts were remembered not so much for their words but more for their successful delivery or not. Throughout the land his subjects sitting tensely on the edge of their chairs, seemingly relaxed from rich Christmas pudding and after-dinner brandies, were in fact agonizingly awaiting his annual message of good cheer, and relaxed only with a sigh of relief and great compassion when their monarch came through without a stumble."

"And, to close, Horst," said Jill, "on another royal announcement, listen to this."
"Long live the Queen!" It was yet another cold, gray day of rain. Packed among a mass of excited patriotic, flag-waving people, I clutched and clung onto a damp, slippery lamp post in Piccadilly Circus as I waited to catch a glimpse of the young Elizabeth II flash by in her golden Coronation coach. Yet, who should capture the hearts of the cheering crowds and worldwide spectators? None other than the lovely 6'6" Queen of Tonga, her white teeth gleaming from her dusky smile, as she insisted on riding through the icy rain in an open carriage.

"Arriving home, weary, yet comforted that I had been part of a slice of actual history in living colour, I was met by a sea of smug smiles. The whole family, along with cousins, aunts and uncles, had watched, warm and comfortable in the cozy living room, the entire show in minute black and white detail on the new television set!"

"Hooray for you, Jill," cheered Horst. Then noticing her close the book and begin to gather up her things, for she was tired, hungry and hoarse, he tugged at her sleeve. "Fair's fair, Jill. I want equal time."

CHAPTER 25

"It was 1951 and I was eighteen years old. I decided to visit my grandparents, Papa's parents, whom I hadn't seen for ten years. Oma and Opa had moved to Hannover at the end of the war to escape the Russians advancing into Berlin. They were forced to flee very quickly in the spring of 1945, taking with them only hand luggage. Their home and life-long possessions were left behind in what would eventually become East Berlin, the Communist zone. They were never able to return. They fled with their daughter, Papa's sister, whose father-in-law lived in Hannover. My grandparents, aunt and her small son, fled by freight train, joining all the other refugees fleeing before the arrival of the Russian troops. They had no time to lose for the very next day the army marched in.

"My rich uncle had died earlier on in the war from a disease more socially-related than to war. His widow, Mama's aunt, and heir to the estate and the business, chose to remain and take her chances. It is reported, somewhat hushed, that she was one of the hundreds of unfortunate women, aged between nine and ninety, who were forced to lie down in the streets of Berlin and be raped by the Red Russian soldiers.

"Aunt Clare had all her documents relating to her possessions safely in Cologne. After the money reformation in 1949, she found herself to be a very wealthy woman again. Although everyone had started out with 40 DM, anyone who still held stocks and shares in companies that restarted business in 1949 under the American occupation, partook in the German economic miracle over the following thirty years.

"In 1946 share certificates of many old established companies were thought to be worthless and were literally thrown away as waste paper into the streets. My clever aunt held on to hers and became one of Europe's millionaires.

"The only way I could travel was by bicycle, having no funds for any other transportation. I had a new three-speed bicycle, the first model of its kind in Germany since the war. It had a steel frame, caliper brakes and was bright blue. I had saved up and bought it out of my wages from what was left of the 50 DM I received every week from my bakery job, after giving Mama 20 DM for housekeeping.

"I decided to take the scenic route from Ludwigshafen to Hannover, a distance of about 300 miles. The autobahns, Hitler's highways, were for motorized traffic only. Those magnificent stretches of roadway had been constructed criss-crossing Germany just before the war in readiness for transportation and fast movement of trucks, troops and supplies. Many of the autobahns could even be closed off to serve as landing strips, providing greater accessibility and speedier movement.

"As I was traveling alone with very little money, I planned to stay in youth hostels and follow Mama's advice 'to eat in small village inns where the food is cheaper and better'. The towns had nothing to offer, anyway, for they were still in the process of being rebuilt.

"Hundreds of cyclists used the side routes in those days, motor cars being a rarity. The journey was very peaceful and safe. My roving eye sought out fellow cyclists of the female sex. After the third day of my ten day journey I met a very attractive girl on whom I spent what little money I had on innocuous pleasures such as soft drinks and ferry boat rides. When we went our separate ways I only had enough money for overnight hostel stays, which meant that I had no money for food and had to survive on a bag of sweets brought from home.

"The routes I took had not been destroyed or even touched by the war. In contrast to my home town, Time had stood still. Many villages had not even seen the advancing American troops as we had.

"The small town where my grandparents lived, Buckeburg, just outside Hannover was one such as those I had passed through. When I arrived I ate and slept for two days. Although the hard journey had been uneventful, I dreaded the return ride. I remembered the signposts indicating that I still had another one hundred miles to go before reaching a certain destination and able to sink into bed. I stayed three weeks with my grandparents whom I had not seen for so very long. We were all a lot older and wiser!

"The father-in-law of my aunt took me for long walks through the woods. He was a forester in East Prussia before leaving for his present home. He would tell me endless stories of deer hunting, (which reminded me of the hunt on my uncle's estate and the stag with the bullet wound in its neck of so many years before)--and how he would chase the many poachers from the Prussian forest back across the Polish border. His living room was a mass of antlers hanging on the walls, each bearing the date of its demise. Even then he was still hunting and I was able to watch him bring in his catch, cut off the huge head, boil it in a cauldron full of water until loosened and fell apart from the skull.

"He died ten years later at the ripe old age of 97. Oma and Opa Schaefer lived into their nineties, both dying of old age within three weeks of each other."

Jill turned to Horst and put her arm around his shoulders. "How lucky you were to have your grandparents live to such a great age. Strange, too, that we both had a grandfather, a ne'er-do-well who died at a comparatively young age."

She switched off the recorder and turned the page of her book and began to read.

"'The 1953 Polytechnic Annual Basketball Banquet, London' is the caption below this black and white official photo, showing a large gathering of young people in their teens and twenties, seated at long white cloth-covered tables, adorned with menus, and awaiting service from the hovering waiters.

"There's me, aged 18," she said. "Not a bad picture of me, good semi-profile showing my beautifully coiffed hairstyle, well-made-up face and chic full-sleeved blouse atop a long black moiré skirt. And there's my friend, Maureen, two seats down. Well, back to the book."

"We had been at the Convent at the same time, but never friendly, being of different ages and running with a different crowd. Maureen was one of the sophisticated girls not athletically inclined. However, we had met up one year after leaving school and found that we had the common bond of both working in the City of London, me at the Bank of England and she with a jewelers company in famous Hatton Garden. We lived closed enough to meet often and travel to work daily on the same train. Most important of all was that we were seekers of young men. At this time especially, we were attracted to the young American servicemen who were stationed all over England.

"How I remember meeting my first American, a tall handsome, curly-haired sailor at a Bournemouth dance hall where I was spending my first holiday without the family at the seaside resort with a Bank girl friend, Shirley. Shirley had become involved with a waiter at the hotel where we were staying and they had invited me along to the tea dance. I wasn't the gooseberry for long as I met Steve whose ship was docked at nearby Weymouth, and enjoyed the rest of my two weeks holiday with him. And, I was hooked!

"Thirty years earlier, Maureen's mother had gone out to California with her two sisters, all Irish girls from Dublin. She had returned alone for a visit when she met and married an Englishman and stayed ever after in England. When I met Maureen, she had been thinking about going out to the U.S.A. to visit her aunts in California. So we schemed and dreamed together.

"But why the basketball dinner of the photo? Well, during our scrimping and saving for the fare money, we decided to improve our minds without any financial cost. So we decided to take an evening class at the Regent Street Polytechnic, close to Piccadilly Circus. The only course convenient to both of us was Beginning Dutch which we attended faithfully for a few classes. I can still say 'Der Tafel ist in der midder von der Etkamer'."

"Well said, mein liebling," said Horst, interrupting. "Did you ever have cause to let someone know that 'the table is in the middle of the dining room'?

"No, but it helped me with my German," she replied tartly. So many words are similar. Now be quiet and listen."

"During one break in this tedious Dutch class, we wandered down to the basketball court, where, to our delight, the local team of Englishmen were playing a team of American players from one of the Air force bases.

"That's why I only got as far as that one Dutch sentence, for we then spent those evenings cheering on the team, rather than uttering guttural sentences. We chatted up the players and went along as supporters on the Poly teams' numerous away games into the forbidden-by-my-father fortresses of the American camps.

"Poor Father! It's just as well he didn't know that every Saturday night that I stayed at Maureen's house, we spent the evening at anywhere in London or the outer suburbs where these lovely young men foregathered. What he didn't know, he wouldn't worry about. Maureen's mother, both understanding and tolerant, had a whispered pact with Mother than I would come to no harm in our dallyings. Mother was a real brick although she was really torn between placating Father and encouraging their only daughter to spread her wings, (although in a direction different to what she would have chosen for me.) But she was the one who since childhood had taken me aside and insisted that as the only two females in a family of six, we had to stand together against those men.

"What a silly-billy I was! Adventurous as it was flaunting family conventions and deceiving disciplinary Father with poor Mother as the go-between, I hadn't deliberately set out on a non-conformist path. I only wanted to fly in my own direction and learn from my own mistakes, even though Father always told me to heed him and not find out about life the hard way. Oh, the trials and tribulations of being the only girl in a family. Needless to say, all my exploits and confrontations with Father were closely watched by the young cousins.

"Not a Saturday night would we pass up to go to Air Force base dances or the glittery, tawdry dance halls of the Hammersmith Palais and London's Lyceum to dance, sip cocktails, chat and generally get acquainted. (I can see Father's point of view there, for they were 'common' places in his eyes, but to me, exciting!) To me this was adult entertainment, so unlike the church social dances or the Saturday night local town hall hops. I'd had enough of sitting sedately with the girls around a cavernous hall, hoping to be invited to dance to the tuneless band by one of the callow youths gathered in a unified group around the exit. Oh no, I preferred being a sophisticated seventeen year old, clad in mature black as I leaned languidly against a pillar or draped myself around a chair, sipping a gin and lime cocktail. I neither sat nor stood in order to avoid the embarrassment of having to slowly unfold myself to the startled stare of an invitation to dance by a shortie!"

Horst roared with laughter. "You can laugh," said Jill. "As a man, you've never been in such a dilemma."

She continued. "Even in one of London's famous pea-soup fogs which went down in history as the densest, filthiest, long-lasting, killer of the old, sick and young, did I venture out, regardless of my parents' dismayed pleas to stay home. Only a fool would venture out in such a peasouper. Yet out I went, clad in thin black glossy raincoat atop my pencil-slim skirt and tight turtle neck sweater. (How Mother despaired of my black garb and begged me to wear something frilly and pastel.) My fine, straight hair, freshly curled under a head scarf was soon limp and lank from the damp chill. With my soon-to-be frozen feet squeezed into a pair of too-small flimsy, fashionable flatties, I left the brightly lit house to enter the dense darkness and grope my way blindly, hand over hand, along the railings and hedges edging the houses down the avenue. With eyes glued to the ground, I made my directionless way across the deserted Common to arrive and meet Maureen at the eerily-lit Underground station. We froze on the desolate platform as we awaited the ghostly train which swooshed into the station, gathered us up into its misty interior and transported us to a suburban station where we were met by a car-load of young airmen.

"We barely made our way through the thick, swirling blanket of whiteness as the car literally inched its way to the dance, guided through the denseness by a scout walking ahead, unable to see even the proverbial finger before his face.

With one fellow guiding the steering wheel and another perched on the front bumper to give warning shouts of any looming objects ahead, we arrived at the dance only to leave shortly afterwards to crawl the same slow way back to catch the last train home!

Horst again roared with laughter. "I really feel for your parents, Jill, having a daughter like you. Only kidding! But seriously, as a father myself, those teenage years are a trial. Goodness only know what I'd have been like – and you too, Jill – if we'd had a daughter. He mused for a moment.

Silence hung heavily in the air. Seated on the top stair of her mother's house, Horst and Jill, surrounded by their past, paused to gather their thoughts. She glanced over at her husband and asked him if she should continue with another story or did he want a turn. Without so much as a nod, he said, "Want to hear about my motor-scooter and why I just had to have one. "I'll tell some facts about post-war Germany on the way." Jill closed the book. He was on a roll!

CHAPTER 26

"I'd had my fill of bicycles so bought on hire-purchase one of the very first motor cycles which came onto the German market after the war, a small Vespa that gave me immense freedom in my pursuit of wine, women and dance!

"Come early Friday afternoon after a very early start in the bakery that morning, I would take off either in the direction of Heidelberg, fifteen miles to the east, or to the spa town ten miles to the west of Ludwigshafen, Bad Durkheim where business was 'as usual' after it's wartime closedown. In fact, business was far more intense than before, for everyone had a lot of living to catch up with! Believe it or not, in those days just post-war, most Germans were slim and lean from their near starvation. Within two years, however, they had eaten and drunk themselves to their present overweight, coupled with a predisposition to heart attacks, an illness unheard of between 1940 and 1948. During the war death was either from bombs, starvation or lack of drugs and medical attention.

"During this post-war period everything was inexpensive—wine, food, services and entertainment. Proprietors had to rebuild the clientele they had lost during the six and a half years of war and the five year post-war period. I remember one cartoon portraying a shopkeeper obsequiously bowing and cloyingly smiling as he said, 'Yes, Frau Miller. Thank you, Frau Miller. At your service, Frau Miller,' words not heard for many a year. The customers' boots were being licked and would continue to be until 1949 when Germany's boom began.

"With the aid of the Marshall Plan whereby Germany, the defeated nation, was granted a huge financial loan by the victorious Americans, Germany was able to get its house in order. German enterprise and hard work enabled every demolished city, businesses and lives to be rebuilt. In retrospect, perhaps Ludwigshafen's devastation was a blessing in disguise, not taking into account, of course, the loss of lives. Like most other industrial cities it was ugly and afforded few recreational facilities. It was rebuilt into a beautiful, modern city that offered all aspects for leisure and enjoyment to the hard-working, hard-playing Germans.

"Many enterprises forced to start afresh with the newest of high efficient machines, created the economic miracle. England in contrast, whose cities were not quite as devastated, were able to continue using their old-fashioned, out-of-date machinery and offered no competition whatsoever to the efficiency of the German factories. By 1950 Germany had no rationing; everything was plentiful and the financial debt paid off. England, on the other hand, the victors with no financial helping hand, had to manage alone. Until 1954 certain items were still rationed."

"Who would have thought," said Jill, a frown on her face, "that the victorious nation would end up the loser, economically, I mean. Doesn't seem fair, does it?"

Horst ignoring her question, smiled weakly, and continued his story.

"One fine Sunday in the middle of 1949 it was announced that the old Reich Mark was to be changed over to the new Deutsch Mark—real money again. Everybody would receive 40 DM.

"Miracle of miracles. Only one week after the change-over the lines in front of the shops and almost all ration cards had disappeared. The shop windows were full of fine food and consumer goods were suddenly plentiful. Where had it all come from? Everybody was supposed to have started with 40 DM. One year later people were driving around in cars. Where had all these things been the previous ten years?

"I had to pass a road test for my motor scooter. I had to return a second time to pass. The examiner refused to examine me the first time because I had a cigarette in my mouth!

"Girls were attracted to men with transportation. The method of informing them was by flashing the keys in the dance hall. The girl, hoping the keys belonged to a car, only found out it was a motor scooter after accepting a ride home on leaving the dance hall. Any transportation was better than a long walk home, the last tram of the day having long since left. Until I had my motor cycle I would carefully screen each dance partner to see how far away she lived and if her attraction was worth a long walk.

"I once walked a girl home some seven miles. She had hoped to meet someone with transportation but had stayed with me throughout the evening because of my charming chatter and dancing expertise. The walk home, however, upset her so much that she planned a very special revenge.

"When we arrived at her house she whispered confidentially in my ear, 'I'll creep upstairs and open my bedroom window.' She went inside her house, blowing me a kiss. I waited in the cold beneath the window. It opened and she called out softly to me, 'Can you creep very quietly?' My enthusiastic reply was, 'Yes, of course.' To which she responded, 'Then very quietly creep home.'

"There was nothing for it. I just had to get a motor scooter!"

Jill burst out laughing, placing one consoling hand on her husband's cheek and reaching for her book with the other. He tried to look tragic beneath his grin and said, "Never say die, though…But wait, Jill, don't you want to hear the rest? I haven't finished. Listen."

"As I've said, a young man with transportation was always successful with the opposite sex. Another successful ruse was to play a musical instrument. There were no juke boxes in the pubs where the young people assembled or any records and players available for purchase.

"I noticed that piano and violin players were greatly adored by the most attractive girls. Since both were too difficult to play, one afternoon I suddenly hit on the idea to rush out and purchase an accordion.

"Now, everyone had only 40 DM to start out with, so Mama was not very keen to help me finance an instrument which might cost 100 DM. To force the issue I went to a music shop and signed a hire purchase agreement for an accordion. I bought a 60 pound instrument, carried it three miles home, lugged it up the eight flights of stairs, and proudly presented it to Mama. She, normally unflustered and placid, turned pale and screamed bitter recriminations at me.

"Yet nothing could stop me. In fact, next day I signed up for expensive music lessons. However, after three weeks and I still was unable to play beautiful melodies to charm the girls, I decided it wasn't for me. I asked Mama to return the instrument. This was absolutely not the done thing in those days. Hire Purchase was a binding contract.

"I carried it half way to the shop and told Mama to stagger on to the store and directed her to 'go cancel all the contract payments on the instrument.' With tears in her eyes, she struggled towards the shop and somehow managed to persuade the owner to take the instrument back. Apparently she berated him for influencing a simple youth to part with his hard-earned money and then placing the burden on his poor mother struggling to make ends meet. The contract was cancelled, but no money was returned.

"Matters didn't rest there. A short while later I decided that ice-skating was the done thing. There was a new ice rink built by the American Forces.

"The idea struck me one morning and by late afternoon I needed ice-skates. So I knew I had to start preparing Mama by noon. By 6 p.m. I had softened her up enough by playing my final card of threatening to join the Foreign Legion. She agreed to accompany me to make a down payment from her hard-earned money, as my wages from the bakery were so meager.

"During the whole four years of Papa's absence, Mama had aged considerably, but never more than during the period of my crazy purchases. My two sisters and young brother never said a word, thinking it better not to make any demands of their own. I, as older brother and at the time father of the family and provider, would soon have squelched any request with energetic arguments and threats. All objections were quickly over-ruled and there was very little sibling contact between us.

"Compared to your full family life, Jill, and growing up with such a large family around you, my youth was very lonely. As the oldest, and a boy, I was rather apart. In fact, hearing what you've read up until now, there's a great similarity between your brother Peter and myself, don't you think?"

"Yes," she replied, "I've thought that often. I know you don't mention your sister much, but I bet she's got a lot of stories about you, her older brother. In fact, I do recall her telling me years ago—when we were better able to converse as my German had improved to the extent that I could hold a conversation with her and share a joke—that she had the same problems with you as I did with Peter. We commiserated with each other over our bullying brothers."

"Go on. I don't believe you. I never bullied her," retorted Horst, quite baffled by the accusation.

"You're just like Peter. He never remembers a thing either." she sighed.

Well, let's get on with the story. At this rate, we're never going to meet!"

"Get a move on then," said Horst huffily. "Pray continue. What's next in the famous saga?"

"Listen, Horst," said Jill. "I was the first of all the sisters' children to be out of school and earning a wage. That is, except for Peter, who was doing his two-year compulsory training in the armed forces, first at an Officer's Training College in

England and then eighteen months in Canada at an Air Force navigation school. He was the first of us to leave home for any period of time.

"The day of his homecoming, Mother, Father, Mike. eight-year old Chris and I drove way out along the Great West Road in the countryside to little London airport, a far cry from the busy airport it is today. We awaited his arrival after his awesome plane ride and long absence from home. None of us, not even Mother and Father, had ever been aloft in the air or even inside a plane, except, of course, for the walk through the incomplete shell of a Spitfire that was on show at Mother's wartime job.

"I remember so well the tall, willowy reed-like figure with small head, with flaxen hair and piercing blue eyes." She paused and turned to Horst. 'Mother once confided in me that when she proudly presented her first born to her mother, Grandma Field's only comment was that his head was so small! Mother was crushed.' She resumed reading, "A handsome, elegant young man in peaked cap and smart blue uniform of the Royal Air Force came into sight. Was this my awful bullying brother? He looked so benign, although his angelic blond looks had always been deceptive! As he descended the moving staircase, he caught sight of us and waved. He greeted Mother and Father with a kiss on the cheek, Mike and Chris a perfunctory pat on the shoulder, and then turned to stare at me in astonishment. Was this his 'useless' younger sister with whom he had gone through so many thicks and thins of growing up, now transformed from an ugly duckling into a surprisingly sleek, shapely, passably pretty dark-haired young lady swan—who he was more than proud to present to his young fellow officers who visited him on leave. They, however, after the wild life of the service and the attractions of Canada and the U.S.A. turned out to be experienced, been-around men. And I wasn't at all what I looked!

"The Four Graces were once again all living close together, which meant a reunification with all the cousins we'd both grown apart from. Peter and I were now completely apart from them, and although closer than ever before to each other, would still remain apart as we each went our own separate ways.

"Aunt Evie's solicitor husband had moved his practice to London. Her three sons, still with their wild country image, were in private schools. The spastic son was living his happy life in a special school. The young daughter, Hilary, the same age as Chris, John and Lollie's daughter, Maureen, was at a local convent school. Lollie's son was ensconced behind his father's shop counter where he stayed many years. Chris, my baby brother, would achieve well academically and follow in Peter's footsteps as an accountant. Mike followed Father into our inherited wine shop. As for the three Lamb girls, Babs the oldest settled for being a secretary and marriage. The middle one, Pat, went to Leeds University to become a teacher and met and married one. The youngest, Valerie, the social fledgling, went to a Finishing School in Switzerland, secretarial school in London, married a doctor and later also went into her father's wine store.

"Of the five shops, the one shared by the unlikely team of Lollie and Evie was soon sold. Bibby and Jack's shop which at the time was the worst of the five, flourished well in its Sloane Square location. Our shop, the only one to have a name change to Martin's Wine and Spirits Stores, also flourished, expanded into a cellar wine bar—and then went plop down the drain with financial difficulties."

Jill put down the book with a rueful smile. "So much for siblings, cousins, bullying brothers…." she said, as Horst added on, "and a bullying son! Well, as for me, I was soon dancing for my life!"

CHAPTER 27

"From 1953 to 1957 Ballroom Dancing was my life, intermingled with my many apprenticeships. Mama and Papa despaired that I would ever settle down to one thing.

"As was customary with German teenagers of a solid middle-class background, ballroom dancing was an entrée into the society of the town in which they lived. To pursue this passion of mine to dance in all the best ballrooms and enter any and every competition, I left home for six months and worked in a bakery in a town which boasted an elegant ballroom in its fine spa hotel. By daylight I baked and by night I danced, snatching a few hours of sleep in the little room provided by the baker.

"I was always exhausted and after I forgot for the third time to put salt in the bread, I was fired. Having no money to return home, the kind old baker loaned me 50 DM which I promised faithfully to repay. I forgot about it and regret that I never did.

"Mama was quite annoyed at my sudden reappearance, though secretly pleased that I had come home. I was always threatening to leave home to join the Foreign Legion if I couldn't get my way. She always gave in, fearing that I would leave for ever.

"Ludwigshafen had a ballroom dance club called the 'Green-White Dancing Club'. My oldest sister, who was very tall, was pleased to have a tall partner like me. She was my first dance partner until I moved on to other girls. I progressed rapidly from partner to partner, always promising each my undying love. The old pitch of 'needing to get closer to you to perfect our partnership' always worked until I moved onto another.

"My sister had only one other partner, a local boy whom the dance master didn't consider of the required social class to be a club member. A powerfully built solid six footer, my sister would say that dancing with him was like partnering a massive tree stump, whereas I was a willowy, thin reed. However, they danced on together, fell in love and got married.

"The dancing competitions were very formal. I wore a dark suit, white shirt and tie, whereas my partner wore a long flowing gown. Yet, how different was this from Papa's dancing days as a young Prussian officer. In his Academy it was mandatory for all officers to learn to dance as they had to attend social affairs. His attire was full dress uniform, jacket buttoned high to his chin, tight trousers and white gloves. When dancing it was not allowed to clasp one's partner behind her back. Only the finger tips could touch and guide.

"I once got carried away during one dance competition. Spinning deliriously to the music of the band, I accidentally trod on the flowing hem of my partner's long gown, flinging her skirtless into the tables, chairs and wine bottles of the vast hall. Red-faced, I had to retrieve my angry, shame-faced partner from the debris and lead her off the floor with her torn skirt wrapped around her legs as the audience laughed and jeered.

"I danced on and on in every competition, making sure never to repeat the careless incident. Always with a new partner, I won many trophies and became a Silver medallist. I never did try for the Gold medal as by that time I had tired of all my apprenticeships which I had endured and completed. I had decided that what I wanted above all was to become an Interpreter. England became my goal. Besides, it was the home of the revered gods of the ballroom—the famous English Ballroom Dancers!

"Still a long way to go, eh Horst, before the fateful meeting? Said Jill. "Meanwhile, while you were perfecting your dancing, I was laying the groundwork for leaving home."

"Yes, perhaps a bit more concentration on ballroom dancing might not have been amiss," teased Horst, well aware of his wife's embarrassment on tripping over his nimble feet on the dance floor.

"To the photo, if you don't mind," retorted Jill huffily.

"Peter, the oldest of we four, with hair still very fair despite the darkening, flattening Brylcreem, had grown to a not surprisingly 6'6". He had two years Royal Air Force navigation training in Canada behind him. Having had his own batman, Peter's Boy Scout neatness was reduced to a bachelor's untidiness. In this colour photo he is portrayed as a lean breaker of hearts and an articled (apprenticed) chartered accountant. Elegantly clad in a dark suit and tie, he is leaning casually against the well-stocked rosewood bar in the drawing room of our home. Both he and it are ready for the 21st Birthday party that evening.

"We had recently moved to Ealing, the Queen of the London suburbs, to a large detached house which stood alone in its own plot in a wide tree-lined avenue. We had left behind the lesser, yet friendlier Chiswick—with is narrower road lined with the semi-detached houses-- of our war years and my early childhood. Left behind too, were our friends. I was not encouraged to continue my friendship with Mary who was coldly told I was not in when she came to call. I was incensed and determined to hang on to my old pals and haunts. But, not for long, for Mother had decided that we were going up in the world.

"On the day of Peter's photograph four years after our move from Chiswick, our imposing red-brick house was ablaze with lights. Under every gabled window of the mock Tudor façade the leaded-light window panes invitingly twinkled to greet the guests to enter from the damp, foggy November night where they were met by Mother and Father at the brightly lit entrance. All was festive at the 'dolls-house'.

"On shedding their warm wraps in the parquet-floored hallway to expose their evening finery, the guests were welcomed into the opened-up expanse of the two main living rooms. There they were greeted by earlier arrivals, the raucous music of a Dixieland jazz band (borrowed by Peter from one of London's cellar clubs) and a welcoming drink! Laughing above the noise, the partygoers of all ages cavorted on the carpet to the rhythm of the brassy band. Some lounged and chatted in the sofa and armchairs while others ate and imbibed in the smoky atmosphere as they watched the nonstop show.

"At a given sign the band struck up the old familiar Happy Birthday theme. With hands and legs held fast in the grips of many eager hands, lanky Peter, the birthday boy, was repeatedly swung up into the air and down to the carpeted floor onto his rear as he received the obligatory twenty-one bumps. Champagne was spilled and glasses clinked as the toasts came thick and fast to keep up with the continuous popping of corks. Father made his congratulatory speech as did all the uncles. Peter extended gracious thanks as he ripped off the gift wrapping from his many presents. Then Mother presented him with a kiss and a huge silver key-to-the-door as a token of his coming of age.

"The reasons for celebration were manifold. As a nation we had survived the bombardments and long austerity of wartime England. As a family it was a time to enjoy the fruits of the recent inheritance. As parents, it was time for Mother and Father to announce the coming of age of their first born, my older brother.

"This will be the party of the season," Mother had previously promised. "We'll invite all the neighbours and, of course, every family member." Yet, Peter's party had another objective, a poorly disguised attempt of Mother and Father to hold me at home. They didn't think me ready to go, or themselves to let me leave. I, aged, eighteen, was the first of the flock to want to leave to pursue my two-year old dream of adventure in the U.S.A.

"After many stormy battles and scenes of bitter tears, my thoroughly and sadly defeated parents had finally agreed that I could go to California for a maximum of one year when I was nineteen. The provisos were that I save up my round-trip fare and a certain sum of money to tide me over until I found a job. They considered these conditions impossible to fulfill, but if they were met, I deserved to go. All their entreaties had fallen on my deaf ears and a stony, determined heart. "Wait until you're twenty-one. You won't be our responsibility then," was Father's hard tone. "We'll miss you terribly, but I do understand," said Mother wistfully, adding "Only I'm afraid there won't be any young men left when you come back." Did she really fear that at twenty-one I would be on the shelf!"

"I was enamored of America, that wonderful land, an alluring beacon shining down from the Hollywood silver screen on a young girl with stars in her eyes! My girlfriend, Maureen, conspirator, ally and sharer of dreams and I, were under the spell of the marvelous American boys in blue, those dashing and charming young Lotharios who were there in their thousands on our tiny isle. We had eyes for no other. We had stringently saved our meager money for two years and in three months time all conditions would be fulfilled! Visas and sponsors had been acquired, passages aboard the Queen Mary ocean liner booked, rooms at our sister convent school reserved in New York, Greyhound cross-country bus tickets paid for, and Maureen's cousins alerted in California for our arrival. My sponsor, acquired through the same Old Girl's bank manager husband, had promised introductions to the Bank of America for employment in Los Angeles. Everything was falling into place. Our Lotusland was in sight!

"As it's your big day, Peter, you may invite anyone you wish. To me Mother had said, "You may select one guest." Mike and Chris, aged 13 and 8, as rest of the family deserved no special consideration. Peter's list was smilingly scrutinized and the invitations sent out. Maureen, my partner-in-crime, was my only choice, but not that of my parents who, although a well-spoken girl of good class, was considered a dubious influence on me. My parents could not conceive that I might be the driving force! However, with Maureen there, their coup de grace may well succeed, for their chances were doubled. Maybe one of us at least, if not both, would be swept off our feet by one of the listed eligibles of handsome young Englishmen and be seduced into forsaking our adventurous schemes and the split-up of our team.

"The social occasion was a brilliant success. The plot failed dismally!"

"Not another cliffhanger ending, Jill, if you don't mind," said Horst in exasperation. "Well, since I know I'll have to wait to find out, it's back to Berlin for me."

CHAPTER 28

"In 1956 my Uncle Herbert collapsed in his bakery in the middle of pulling out some bread from the oven. His wife, my Aunt Marie, telephoned Mama and pleaded for me to come to Berlin and run the bakery for about two months while her husband had his stomach operation. I was only too glad to agree, for I was in between jobs, and Berlin sounded adventurous. I had not been back to the city of my birth since the year we left in 1939, just before the outbreak of the war. This was partly because of the intervening war years and the long distance from Ludwigshafen, but mostly from lack of funds and transportation.

"The last time I had seen Oma Schaar and my aunt and four cousins was on the farm in Bavaria when Uncle was a prisoner of war in Russia. When he returned his spirit and health were broken from mal-treatment and malnutrition at the hands of brutal Russians. The treatment of German prisoners by the Russians was, in a sense, understandable for the Nazis had slaughtered twenty million Russian soldiers on the Russian front.

"Uncle told me the story of his capture. He was part of a machine gun crew behind Russian lines with the famous MG42 which could shoot thousands of rounds per minute. Crews were spread out spasmodically within a fifty mile area and when the Russians attacked in twenty waves of 30,000 men, they would mow them down with the machine guns. The MG42's muzzle had to be exchanged every ten minutes as it became red hot from constant firing. The muzzle was exchanged continuously. Along the fifty mile stretch bodies piled high and succeeding waves of attacking Russians, who were poorly armed with one rifle to every five men, would pick up arms from their fallen comrades, using the dead bodies as a human wall as protection against the deadly machine guns. Using their protective device, the Russians were finally able to breach the German lines and Uncle was one of the soldiers captured. He was taken prisoner to a camp in Russia where he remained for many years.

"Now he had his stomach trouble and I was called to Berlin. Ready and keen to go, with little preparation, I jumped on my motor scooter and traveled towards the eastern part of Germany which had been delegated to the Russians by the Allies at the end of the war. In 1956 there was no Wall and it was easy to cross over the border. Berlin, being situated in the center of the part of Germany controlled by Russia, could only be reached by traversing through this territory.

"Halfway into the zone I stopped to check a minor defect on my scooter. Within a minute I was surrounded by three Volkspolizei, a People's Police motor cycle squad of four who questioned my motives for stopping in their glorious Democratic Republic of Germany. Satisfied that I was harmless, they allowed me to proceed into the Western sector of Berlin where my uncle's bakery was located.

"When I arrived I had time only for a cup of coffee before I started work. The shop was empty of wares and I had to bake everything from scratch without any helpers since Uncle had no employees. After working day and night for three continuous days, I had filled up the bakery and decided it was time to explore Berlin. As usual, I gave up my sleep and sought my pleasures by night.

"I visited a dance-hall in the center of West Berlin, a place which became famous in the Roaring Twenties for its innovative way of 'invitation to the dance'. Each table around the huge dance floor displayed a lighted telephone number and a telephone which the clientele would use to put forward requests to dance, drink or chat!

"I duly invited a pleasant young Berlin woman to dance, drink and chat. At 2 a.m. she requested to be escorted home. Unfortunately she lived across the border in East Berlin, yet there was no problem as access to and fro was simple. Off we went on my scooter through the gaily lit streets of West Berlin, crossed over the Checkpoint into East Berlin where civilization suddenly seemed to have disappeared. That part of the city was in darkness, desolation and loneliness. The empty street was lined with buildings crumbling into decay and with rubble from the war, still strewn around.

"East Germany, delegated to the Russian victors by the Allied Powers of the U.S.A, England, France and Russia, had been picked clean of any materials by the Russians to use in rebuilding their own country. A revenge in part, perhaps, for they took every nail, machine and tram car and even dismantled the rails. It would be sixteen years later when Communist Russia had integrated the East

German territory into their own empire that they realized it was to their benefit to encourage East Germany to rebuild and produce.

"Contrary to my usual idea of escorting and spending some time with a girlfriend, I stopped my scooter outside her ramshackle apartment building, bid her goodnight and turned around quickly in the direction of the lighted streets of West Berlin with its happy, well-dressed people, neon-lit shop windows and noisy traffic. I felt a thousand miles away from that type of world.

"I drove through endless drab, dark streets still in ruins from the bombs, trying to find my way back to the Checkpoint. There was not a soul around to ask the way. Everyone stayed home, for there was nothing to do after dark and nowhere to go.

"Suddenly a hundred yards away from me I saw the glow of the street lights of West Berlin on the horizon. I am not at all religious, yet when I approached the glitter of that part of the city, I whispered my deep gratitude to my Maker that I had arrived out of the sinister, frightening decay of East Berlin. I swore never to return to the East. However, thirteen years later I did return. The Checkpoint Charlie was then a purpose-built barrier, a gap in the ugly, towering dividing Wall. Nothing had changed in appearance except the rubble had gone and buildings patched up. However, the same darkness, gloom and empty streets remained with its sad-faced, poorly-dressed people."

Jill stared at her husband for she had never heard this revelation before. Yet she could well visualize the story for she had accompanied him on that return visit thirteen years later.

"Why didn't we go to the famous dance hall when we were in Berlin, lieb? she decided to ask.

"Well, to be quite honest, I had completely forgotten about it until you brought all this history stuff up." Jill knew from his tone that he was not admonishing her for she could see that he was quite enjoying unearthing his past. "Besides, I was too busy with business," he added as an afterthought.

Jill was fingering a birthday card shaped like a key, its cardboard bent and corners dog-eared, the shiny silver also a little tarnished. Horst had never seen before seen such a strange-shaped greeting card.

Jill began to relate, first explaining that the key story would explain the cliffhanger at the end of the 21st Birthday party. "The plot to keep me in England had failed, as I told you. This key was a symbol of my freedom, I suppose." She opened her book and flipped through the pages. "Here's a passage about the key."

"In a friendly California beach town, one of the small, cozy furnished apartments in the pink stucco building was cooling down after the heat of the hot February day.

"A few intimates, casually dressed in the current style of jeans and T-shirts, were gathered together in the flickering candlelight around a worn coffee table. An assortment of cracked dishes filled with avocado dip and barbeque chips covered the table top. The soft background hi-fi music was interrupted by the Happy Birthday song sung by my roommates as we raised our glasses of sparking California wine to give the toast. Embraces replaced the childish bumps.

"Excitedly I opened the colourfully-wrapped presents and thanked my guests. Then last but certainly not least, I tore the brown paper off the family present from England. It was the camera, so carefully selected and lovingly sent from so far away—the one I had hinted at. Tearfully I opened the card Mother and Father had airmailed with love from everybody—my brothers, aunts, uncles and cousins. It was symbolically-shaped silver key to the front door.

"More than two years had passed since that other celebrated party, time spent slowly, surely and hopefully acquiring the maturity and wisdom required to meet the deadline of this birthday—my 21st.

"I made a spur of the moment long distance phone call to greet and thank them all at the family breakfast table. 'Yes, yes, my thanks and all my love to you. Yes, I'm well. Everything okay your end? Yes, I'll be coming home soon!'

"But, as of then, I was twenty-one, had come of age, yet still had a long way to go!"

She closed the book. "And when I finally made that trip home, how things had moved on with all the family," said Jill "As you know, I turned up unannounced and nobody was home. Well, Bibbie's oldest daughter with the golden curls celebrated her twenty-first birthday two days later. Of course, I was invited to the sumptuous occasion, so reminiscent of Peter's party eight years before. Bibbie and Jack's wine store had done exceedingly well and they were well able to indulge the whims of their three daughters and only son."

Leafing through the book, she came across the passage. "Everyone was invited as before. The Lamb girls, one with her boyfriend, the middle one down from university with her fiancé and the madcap youngest of the bright blue eyes, and a dear younger sister to me since her visit to San Francisco with Mother. Lollie and Spence with teenage son and younger daughter were there, as were the Country Cousins. Auntie Evie, widowed a year, after Sydney's heart attack and the loss of a lucrative law practicing husband, had turned her large home into a genteel boarding house for retired gentlemen, one of whom she married within a year. Her boys, our wild country cousins, were settling down. The oldest entered his stepfather's business. The second son, a nineteen year old, had recently met and married a seventeen year old model and were awaiting their first child. No longer little, the spastic son was leading a happy existence in a special home. The youngest son and only daughter were at fee-paying schools."

"And as for my brothers," she said, turning to her husband, "Well, Mike, still very serious and quiet, was with Father in the family business. And Peter, on the morning of Barbara's party rushed in waving a letter announcing that he had finally passed his Accountancy exam on his third attempt. Latin, of all subjects, had repeatedly let him down!" She chuckled at the memory. "I well remember congratulating him with a tight hug around his neck, and how pleased, and surprised, he was at my gesture, our first real contact since the magazine hand-in-hand photo of twenty years before."

She paused and closed the book. "Phew, that was quite an emotional moment, Horst." He nodded and stroked her hand, then reached for a greetings card that had fallen down from inside the card during her account. He handed it to her with a quizzical expression on his face for it said 'Merry Christmas Grandmother' announced by a startled gray-eyed orange fluffy ball of a kitten popping Jack-in-the-Box style out of a beribboned box.

Jill, failing to recognize it, opened it, and immediately saw the familiar handwriting of years of recent correspondence between herself and Eileen.

Inside Eileen had written 'Ignore the term Grandmother. The card was too adorable to resist! Heaven only knows where either of us will be this time next year—but Merry Christmas to the best roommate I could ever have. All my love, Eileen." In the bottom left hand corner was the date of December 1958.

Eileen was her old friend with whom she had shared her San Francisco apartment those last two years before returning home to England. Little five foot two with big eyes of blue, whose prim school-marmish clothes and boyish figure belied her feminine charms, much to Jill's chagrin. For herself it had been vice versa. Eileen had more books on her shelves and packed away in suitcases than Jill had clothes in her bulging wardrobe.

A casual acquaintance of her Convent school days in London, they had become reacquainted at an Old Girls meeting on Jill's leave of absence from her secretarial job with the Beauty Pageant in Southern California. Their friendship had ripened into a strong and lasting relationship. Eileen joined Jill shortly afterwards in San Francisco, that wonderful city of their maturing years. It was there that they had finally been able to shed their Convent school shackles to blossom out gloriously in love with the world.

Mutt and Jeff, the long and the short of it, they were called by all. Jill even took Eileen along on a Tip-Topper Tall Club's ski trip to Squaw Valley. There they'd spent the weekend either floundering helplessly in a laughing heap in the snow or driving the gigantic members of the club, all between six and seven feet plus, to distraction by their endless playing of Sinatra's current 1957 hit 'Witchcraft' on the juke box in the log cabin hotel.

Jill remembered what a pint-sized poppet she had felt as she actually stretched tall for the first time in her life to acquire the extra inch to become eligible to join the club.

Little Eileen, although distraught that Jill was not returning to San Francisco, unexpectedly flew to London for her roommate's wedding day. Eileen adored literature, learning, men and cats—and not necessarily in that order!

With a far-away look on her bemused face, Jill put the card in the pocket of her cardigan, and whispered to Horst, "This I certainly want to keep."

Horst, studying intently another photo, ignored her whisper. "Well, well, this will bring us up to date, I think," he said, showing it to Jill.

The black and white photo showed a bald-headed man standing high above a crowd of people with their backs to the camera. The speaker, leaning against a sign which says 'The Conservative and Unionist Party' is talking down to an argumentative onlooker. In the background under the leafy trees is a young Irish-looking man with a shock of dark, unruly hair. Pantomiming with his hand to his mouth, he is either entertaining the bemused Sunday crowd or imparting his views on the current Irish situation.

It is London's famous Speaker's Corner where anyone may ascend a soapbox to expound his views to whomsoever will linger and listen.

"I remember all the events leading up to that day so well. Turn on the tape," he urged.

CHAPTER 29

"It was May 1959 and my entire family had assembled, Mama, Papa and my younger sister with her husband and small son. My seventeen year old pretty, blond sister—and my younger brother, aged 15, a younger version of me," he added with amusement, "were also present.

"All day long Mama had made extra trips up and down the long flights of stairs to the apartment, bringing in beer and wine in readiness for the party that evening. I was about to leave for foreign lands—the first one of the family to venture away from home and out of Germany. That is, except for Papa who had been a prisoner-of-war in France after the war. I was off to England for three months to perfect my English. To be an English interpreter had been my undying desire for the previous six months. My pending departure deserved a good send off as I'd depleted my parent's patience that I would ever settle into one occupation.

"We had started the merry-making at 5pm as everyone got home from work that Friday evening. And as the train traveling across Germany, Belgium and France left at midnight, it meant that the goodbye party lasted six hours." Horst gave Jill a meaningful look as he stressed the duration of the celebration.

"By that time we were all very sad. Papa was in tears, though it didn't take much for sentimental Papa to weep. Even a sweet-sounding operetta caused his tender heart-strings to twang. I almost decided to discard my plans and stay at home with the family who were obviously desolate at my departure. I do think, though, that they would have carried me to the train if I had voiced any such doubts.

"When it came time to leave, I waved up to everyone hanging out of the living room window and called out, "I'll be back in three months, September at the latest. I don't want to miss the Wurstmarkt!

"No true-blooded German in that southwest part of Germany where we lived, would forego the annual wine festival. It was held in the famous spa town of Bad Durkheim, twenty miles from our Rhein Valley town of Ludwigshafen with its rich, chemical factories and powerful stink. Besides, I'd promised my girlfriend that apart from behaving myself while away in foreign lands, I would be back for the week's fun." Horst and Jill exchanged an intimate smile. "Inside the massive tents," he continued, "where the brass bands played, strangers become instant friends after a few hours of non-stop wine, ending up embracing, swaying arm-in-arm, or shunkeling, to the blaring music and dancing atop the long wooden tables, around which thousands of participants sat for hours on end.

"My brother came on the tram with me to Mannheim station where he left me with a quick hug, wished me luck and caught the next tram back home. By this time I was feeling quite unwell and had to contend with a train full of European holiday makers all going to the Belgian port of Ostend, either to disembark along the route or proceed, as I was, across the English Channel to Dover in England.

"It was a dreadful ten hour train ride, as I sat crushed inside the crowded train, sleeping fitfully and fertilizing the countryside from an open window in the narrow corridor! When the train finally arrived at the Belgian port, I gladly joined the throng of passengers who pushed from all sides in their haste to join the long line to embark on the four hour crossing to England.

"I slept through the entire rocky crossing in the massive, oily-smelling ferry boat, loaded to the hilt with other passengers who had embarked at Ostend, as it churned its way the twenty-two miles across the water. Little did I know that this crossing was to be the first of so many more over the next fifteen years.

"Well," interrupted Jill, "I'd only done the crossing once before I met you, liebling, and that was on a school exchange visit to a French student's home. I was seasick, too." She had lost count of the Channel crossings they had undertaken together during the past decades to visit each other's family in England and Germany.

Horst continued. "I dimly remember arriving at London's Victoria train station some fifteen hours later, exhausted, groggy and unfresh with only a vague idea of London. An acquaintance in the know had told me to go to North London where I would find cheap accommodations. So I jumped on a north-bound, strange-looking, red double-decker bus with my two suitcases and uneaten sandwiches, so lovingly prepared by Mama many hours and miles behind me. I asked the uniformed conductress in my halting English, "Where cheap room, please?"

"Oh yeah," she replied. "Camden Town. That's a good place to look. There's a big notice board with 'Rooms to Rent' advertised. She told me where to alight and pointed me in the direction of a newsagent shop where I found the board covered with lots of little postcards. Among the many interesting items for sale or hire, I noticed quite a few French ladies willing to give lessons. I read the section of 'Rooms Available to Rent'. The cheapest one attracted my attention. I took down the address.

"With my strength failing fast, I struggled another mile up the seedy road to an old shabby four-storey house with peeling paint and crumbling bricks. I knocked on the shaky door and requested a room of the landlady in curlers, cloth bedroom slippers and tatty robe. She eyed me-- a tall, dirty, haggard-looking young foreigner—with suspicion. "Yeah, I 'ave a room. Aint very comfy. "ow long fer, ducks?"

"She pointed out that the room was dark, cold, on the top floor under the roof and had no running water; the toilet and bathroom facilities were shared by the other tenants. There were no cooking facilities except one gas burner on the landing outside—and all food must definitely be kept in tins away from the foraging mice.

"I took the room. The price was right and I wanted to sleep. I had saved long and hard for over a year to make this trip and a little bit of squalour wasn't going to deter me. Perhaps I'd look for something better later on. Anyhow, I didn't have much money on me, having left my savings behind with Mama who would send me allotments every month. The money never did arrive in time of need, of course.

Jill laughed. She remembered how years later she found out that Horst pawned his treasured electric shaver to take her on a dancing date shortly after their meeting.

"Well," he continued, "I slept fitfully, squeezed into a too-short, narrow bed with damp, unpleasant-smelling gray sheets under the sloping roof of the very perfunctorily decorated and furnished attic. The woolen blankets, too, were so different from the fluffy eiderdown comforter I was used to.

"Next morning after fourteen hours of unconsciousness, I awoke to a glorious Sunday. Exploration of foreign territory was my first thought.

"I walked for five miles, passing houses whose red bricks and slate tiled roofs were strange to me. Traffic traveled on the wrong side of the road, bounded by shops with unfamiliar displays and, of course, everyone spoke a foreign language!

"My destination was the famous 'Speaker's Corner' in London's Hyde Park, where I found it exceeded all the glowing reports I had ever read about it. People, noise, crowds and masses, all dressed up for the Sunday-morning-only show—all shapes, sizes, colours of skin and nationalities. For the very first time I saw a large group of Negroes, Indians and Pakistanis, all assembled in native dress around the speaker of their own race.

"I wandered from soap box to soap box and speaker to speaker, taking in all the unfamiliar, exciting sights. I listened to the yells, screams and heckles of the hustling, bustling crowds as they moved on, bemused and silent, or vociferous and animated.

"The pretty English girls didn't escape my attention, although I intended my stay to be devoid of such pleasures. To find a language college and to study hard was my plan.

"How different the girls looked from the German girls. They were slimmer, taller, well-dressed in the latest modern 'with-it' styles and wearing lots of eye makeup and bright lipstick. To me they looked as if they had stepped out of a fashion magazine."

Jill remembered how she had stood out from the blond beigeness of the people in the crowded tram carrying her to her job in Heidelberg. Her pink skin, lively blue eyes and rosy lips, all enhanced with makeup, had contrasted with the tired pallor of the broad-shouldered, unadorned German women.

Horst glanced at Jill as he continued. "I did notice one very tall, dark-haired girl, dressed in blue, and was tempted to talk to her. But she disappeared into the crowd.

"After another half hour I decided to move on from the unintelligible garble and strange accents of the soapbox speakers and away from the noise of the heckling crowds. It was time to make my way to the many other interesting tourist sights of London awaiting me.

"I looked for a quiet place to sit and study my map of London. A short distance away, yet still within sight of the rowdy scene, I noticed a folding wooden chair alone on the grass. I went over to it and sat down, hesitatingly, not knowing if it belonged to anyone. Or, far worse, I worried that a park-keeper would come along and demand some of my carefully rationed money! I bent down over the map spread out on my knees and began to study it."

This memory made Horst laugh. "That was the start of it all, wasn't it?" He noticed Jill fingering her book, and smiled. "I bet you've got something about our meeting in your book."

"Of course! And a good follow-up to your story. Want to hear it? I know I've got the piece I wrote about the photo somewhere," she said, rummaging leaf by leaf through the book. "I'll read it if you like, though I do remember it's a bit personal," she added shyly. Horst nodded, his interest piqued.

CHAPTER 30

"I remember that lovely hot Sunday in May," began the preamble to their chance meeting. "May 1959 and just twenty-four years old," read Jill. "I remember the scent of the air, the light breeze touching the hair on my cheeks and the warm spot on my shoulder as I walk spiritedly along with the sun on my back. That uplifting stimulation of the senses that invokes in me a lightness of spirit, a tug at the heart and an elation at just being there at that very moment as I move forward into the unknown immediate future—a wonderful heady feeling. Such were my thoughts as I set out on that warm, sunny, memorable Sunday morning in London, just three weeks home after a five year absence.

"Feeling elated with life, the world, myself and everyone, I had returned for the proverbial second visit home before deciding to settle down abroad. Five years had passed since waving goodbye in 1954 from the deck of the Queen Mary as it sailed from Southampton to New York. My friend and travel mate had long since parted. The ties of our friendship, so weakly cemented by the single bond of our achieved goal, had broken. I had whispered au revoir to a glistening San Francisco beneath me on its seven hills, as the plane turned in the brilliance of a new day on its nineteen hour flight via the North Pole to London. For one brief moment I wondered how long it would be before I would return to the lovely city which for two years had been my home full of laughter and tears and with good friends awaiting my return. Goodbye Lee of the Tiptoppers. Thanks for everything. Goodbye Eileen. Yes, heaven only knows where we'll be this time next year!" She paused and looked over at her husband, who smiled and encouraged her to continue.

"The flight home had been on the spur of the moment, although I'd had it in mind since New Year 1959. On my arrival at London Airport I took a taxi home to the doll-house across the road. No-one was home! Mother and Father were at a school sport function for my baby brother, fourteen year old Chris. Auntie Bibbie espied me from her house across the road and welcomed me home. Over a cup of tea she told me how much Mother had missed me and seemed surprised when I disbelieved her. I had never known! Although when Mother had visited me in San Francisco the previous year with Auntie Bibbie's youngest daughter as her travel companion, I had felt a twinge of jealousy at their fond relationship. I realized what I had sacrificed to gain my independence and self-esteem in my own way.

She again turned to Horst with a flushed face. "Well, I did warn you it was kinda personal." He smiled once more and told her to continue.

"The day of my arrival in early May, the sun shone in London for the first time that year. It continued blazing down hot and bright through to an Indian summer at the end of September. A record summer that would go down in history as 'That Summer of '59'. And, I did remember thinking that the English climate wasn't so bad after all! Little did I know that in early October when a cool breeze came up and dark clouds loomed overhead, I would remark that 'winters were quite chilly!' "Winters!" came the reply. "It's not winter yet. Just you wait!" Would I have turned and run had I known that I was soon to be in the midst of the coldest winter of the century and how I would cry tears of joy the following spring on seeing a delicate crocus push its yellow head through the frozen snow of the previous five winter months?"

She skipped a couple of pages, feeling a little foolish for revealing such personal details. "I'm going to cut right to the chase. This is where it really starts, in fact where we finally catch up with each other."

"That warm Sunday morning, feeling like a tourist myself, I had decided to take the train up to Hyde Park Corner to be entertained by the soap-box orators at Speaker's Corner. Dressed in my blue pedal-pusher pants, sweater and moccasins, I set out happily in the bright sunshine and crossed over the grass to join the throngs. As I wandered from group to group, I sized up any interesting young males. I noticed one tall, thin young man in his mid twenties, dressed in a brown leather battle-dress style jacket, smart trousers, brushed-back hair with a soft quiff—and leather sandals. He looked neither English nor American, especially with those sandals! Anyway, I lost sight of him.

"I mingled with the crowd, laughing along and listening to the heckling. As I moved from group to group, keeping on the fringe, I suddenly found myself at the end of the show with an expanse of grass stretching before me. That's when I espied him again. Sitting way off in the middle of the grass on a rental chair, he was intently studying something on his lap.

"I hesitated to approach and began to turn back into the crowd, when an inner voice stopped me. It said, "If you don't go over to him, you might regret it the rest of your life!" As if my head was in the grip of a tight vice around, I was turned around and drawn by a magnetic force across the grass, eyes down to the ground, hands to my side, seeing only the grass and patches of earth, until my eyes rested on those sandals. On glancing up, my eyes met a pair of startled round blue eyes, wavering and wondering if I had come to claim the chair. He jumped quickly to his feet and proffered me the chair. I quickly gained my composure, waved aside the offer, smiled, extended my hand and introduced myself.

"He, grateful that he was not in the wrong, explained in halting English that it was his first day in London after leaving his home in Germany the day before. He was planning his day's sight-seeing in London and was wondering where to start. Although a native of the city, I told him that I, too, felt like a tourist after five years absence. He suggested we sight-see together.

"We walked the length and breadth of London, enjoying each other's company and the sights of London. By mid-afternoon we looked for a pub to get a drink, but London's licensing laws closed them down between three and six o'clock. I suggested we hop on the underground train and go to my house for a cup of tea.

"When we walked in Mother and Father were very hospitable, although a little nervous as they were awaiting a prospective buyer to view the house. Mother had made an offer on a house across the road and was eager to sell. Not only nervous, but excited too, for the persons coming to see the house were none other than the famous singing duo who had recently won the Eurovision Song Contest that year. This meant nothing to me but greatly impressed Horst who had watched the competition on television in Germany. Well, they didn't turn up that afternoon and the sale fell through. (Mother, however, was still determined to sell and during the next six weeks our chore was to shine up the stainless steel sink in the kitchen whenever a buyer was expected.)

"On that day, though, we sat around over a cup of tea chatting, followed by glasses of sherry and cocktails. My brother, Mike, who was working in a local hospital as an orderly at the time, a job assigned him because his pacifist views prevented him from doing his compulsory two-year National Service in the army, was friendly and interested in his sister's new friend. In fact he and Horst became so friendly that Mike was asked to be best man at the wedding.

"As the evening drew to a close, Horst said that he would have to be on his way as next day he was going to start looking for a language school. Mike offered to drive him to the station in his open car, and I went along. Noticing that I was getting chilled, Horst took off his leather jacket and draped it around my shoulders. He declined it when he got out at the station, saying that he would get it another time.

"I knew then that I would see him again soon!" Jill closed the book. "What a great start to a wonderful year that was," she sighed happily.

CHAPTER 31

Jill pulled from her pocket a little piece of newspaper she'd stuffed there earlier that day in the attic.

"We looked at this LONDON ROMANCE article earlier this evening. We never did find out who put that announcement in the Daily Standard, did we?" she said, handing the news article to Horst.

"Yes, we did, or at least I knew," he replied. "It was your brother Mike. I thought you knew all this time. I got it out of him shortly after our wedding. I'm sure I understood correctly, although my English was somewhat shaky at the time."

Surprised at the revelation that her brother had announced their engagement to all of London, and that the prestigious newspaper had considered it newsworthy, Jill said with a smile, "How surprised we were that hot day when the photographer turned up to take our photo and how we rushed around to make ourselves presentable. What a summer that was!"

Jill and Horst had decided on the spur of the moment to get engaged on their homeward-bound train journey from central London after viewing the thrilling spectacle of the Trooping of the Colour ceremony. Under a cloudless blue sky, the brilliant sun shone down onto the colourful pageant. Queen Elizabeth on horseback, dressed in her uniformed finery of rich velvet cloak and plumed hat, led her clip-clopping Horseguards down the tree-lined Mall from Buckingham Palace to the spacious parade grounds, all to the accompaniment of brassy music from the marching bands and the cheers of the pavement-packed spectators.

On their arrival back at Jill's home, her mother and father had just returned from church and were awaiting the aunts, uncles and cousins from across the avenue for the customary Sunday 'sherry' social gathering. When the couple casually announced their news, at first, there was a stunned silence, (they had only known each other one week). Then cheers of delight erupted, followed by much champagne-cork popping to toast the happy couple.

In fact, Jill's parents really took the news very well. They hadn't known what to expect of their daughter who had suddenly turned up after living abroad for so long. Her mother seemed especially pleased that at long last her daughter had met someone who would keep her 'this side of the Atlantic'. Her father, on the other hand, although impressed with the formal asking for his daughter's hand in marriage, did not question the couple's plan to settle in Germany. It was traditional, at that time, to live in the husband's homeland. His main concern was that his daughter be kept in the traditional manner to which she was accustomed and became disconcerted when Jill explained the modern way. She was prepared to support her penniless student husband until completion of his studies by seeking secretarial employment at one of the many American military bases in Germany.

Her aunts and uncles and all her younger cousins, in their teens and early twenties, feted the happy couple with invitations to tea and to dine. They were curious to know more about the tall, thin, handsome young German whose deep voice and halting English had charmed and captured the heart of Jill, the oldest girl of the clan. In fact, he had charmed them all, especially Mother who insisted that he immediately leave his squalid attic room in Camden Town on the wrong side of London and move into the family home in the Queen of the Suburbs.

Nobody knew where Ludwigshafen was. Pronouncing it was even difficult, especially for Mother who had endless trouble getting her tongue around the syllables. Even had they been told it was near Mannheim and on the River Rhein, it wouldn't have made any difference. France, especially the Riviera, was where they all spent their summer holidays. Peter did make one rather startling announcement that fazed nobody but the older generation who had gone through the war and caused Horst's eyebrows to raise slightly. "Why, yes, of course, Ludwigshafen is one of the cities we practiced bombing, on paper, of course, during my navigation training in the Air Force!"

The wedding was planned for the end of July, five weeks away. This created excitement and euphoria because it caught everyone up in the frantic preparations, and what a social occasion for the bride-to-be's parents. Jill and Horst spent the time getting better acquainted as they shared the warm summer evenings strolling through the fields and woods of nearby Gunnersbury Park. She learned about his life and home in Germany, a country she had never visited. He learned to perfect his English and never needed to enroll in a Language School!

The war, long over for fourteen years, didn't concern them any more except for a few hazy memories. Yet, from the few stories Horst had told, Jill could see that his family's hardships had been many. Young teenage Horst and his mother had been the sole support of the family of three younger siblings during his father's imprisonment. Her war years in England were trivial compared to his in Germany.

It was only after much cautious probing so as not to offend him, did Jill, although slightly chagrined, yet relieved, learn that Horst's cut-off thumb was the result of a careless accident rather than brutal torture at the hands of some sadistic, goodness-only-know who during the war!

"Yes, what a summer that was," sighed Jill, happily. "You know, Horst, you've never told me how you broke the news to your parents about us, apart from the stupid postcard describing me as a blond."

"Quite simple, liebling. I wrote one brief letter saying that I was going to get married. And that was that. Mama responded saying that she and Papa hoped I knew what I was doing, being in a foreign country, and so on. Next thing they received the wedding invitation and Mama said she would be over with my youngest sister. That's all there was to it. Can't remember sending a postcard."

"Alright. Now this next page reveals my thoughts on meeting Mama, said Jill, " when she arrived for our wedding. Now, this is something you've never heard before." Horst looked anxious and curious.

"Don't worry," reassured Jill. "It's nothing dreadful at all. Ready?"

"I remember so well," read Jill, "first meeting Mama. We had driven up to London's Victoria Station on yet another hot, beautiful day of continuous sunshine, to meet her and the younger sister from their Rheinland home.

"While waiting for her to alight from one of the many carriages of the boat train arriving from Dover, we looked for her among the swirling masses of passengers, all weary from the fifteen hour train and boat journey. Loaded down with suitcases, they rushed about gabbling in many tongues as the eagerly left the cavernous railway station of smoky smells, snorts and whistles, to disperse into the soon-to-be called Swinging London of the Sixties.

"There she is," yelled Horst excitedly as he rushed forward to meet her as she stepped down from the train. I remained in the background, waiting to be brought forward and introduced.

"I saw a small, middle-aged woman, a little on the dumpy side, dressed unobtrusively in plain drab clothing, travel weary and disheveled. Her heavy-lidded eyes sat in a round kind face, smooth and beige in its unpainted summer tan. Her broad shoulders sat on a plump back that tapered down to trim hips, well-shaped legs and neatly-turned ankles. I would often see this shape in Germany. Whereas English women tend to become pear-shaped, German women become more like an inverted triangle.

"Accompanying her was Horst's pretty, seventeen year old blond sister, with the modern pixie hair-style of Jean Seberg, the current starlet from Hollywood who had been chosen to play Joan of Arc. This sister became quite an attraction for all the Englishmen, old and young alike. I noticed how the wives and girlfriends tightened their grip on their partner's arm whenever this sister was around!

"This meeting on that hot day in July 1959 not only introduced me to my future mother-in-law, but also to the first-hand observance of the intimate embrace between mother and son, the bear hug of the Continentals—the wide-enfolding of loving arms, the exposure of full-frontal faces with endearing murmurs and mutually comforting back-patting. How different from the cool, quick greeting, to which I was accustomed, of the perfunctory peck of tight lips on a side-swept cheek with hands shyly held at arms length, so fleetingly and timidly allowed to touch."

Jill peeked at Horst, who grinned sardonically. "Not only is that a good description, but also another of your 'coming up for air' sentences."

"Well, let me finish this paragraph." she retorted, reading. "However modified in duration or intensity this embrace may be, depends upon the participants and the occasion. At that moment, though, I had witnessed the ultimate expression of love and caring." Horst smiled at his wife's compliment.

"Remember, too, Horst, what Mama confided to you about me?" asked Jill. "She said that she was impressed with how I stayed in the background and didn't rush forward with you. You thought that a great compliment to me from your mother. But what else could I have done? My polite English upbringing, and my personally cultivated reticence, did not predispose me to rush in where 'angels fear to tread', she said, wagging her finger. "Mothers sometimes, Mother Nature seldom, but mothers-in-law never, were to be fooled with anywhere, anytime. And anyhow, I wanted to give you the opportunity to have an intimate meeting and", she added with a laugh, "the opportunity for me to size her up, as well as the situation, from a safe distance. Final word, Horst, I also didn't speak any German!"

Horst laughed his head off. "Well, goodness only knows how long we've been sitting here on these stairs," said Jill. "It's getting quite dark and I'm beginning to feel rather stiff."

"We must have been up here for hours," said Horst. "How time flies when you get carried away."

"And having fun," finished up Jill. "We're getting to the end of the book. Look here's the newspaper announcement that says, 'The wedding of Jill, only daughter of Mr. And Mrs. R.J. Martin, and Horst Schaefer of Ludwigshafen on Rhine, will take place on July 26 at St. Dunstan's Church at 3 p.m.'

"This will be the wedding of the season," said Mother. "We'll invite all the neighbours and friends, and of course, every family member. The three Field sisters and spouses, four Martin sisters with spouses, the two Martin brothers and spouses—and cousins galore! The neighbours from down the road, next door, from church and the outspoken one from across the road who'd bluntly asked if the happy couple had 'to get married'. To which, I remember with great glee, Mother answered earnestly, '"Good gracious, no. They haven't known each other long enough!'

"Our imposing house was ablaze with sunshine. It was a hot July day and a wedding reception was taking place. On arrival at the church, the guests dressed in wedding finery, were welcomed into the opened-up expanse of the two living rooms, and greeted by the receiving line of parents-of-the-bride, the bride and groom, the mother and sister of the groom, and brothers of the bride. Offered a drink of sherry from a silver tray proffered by the family retainers (Mother's cleaning woman and husband acting as barman and waitress), the guests were ushered in to enjoy the catering at the adept hands of Mason Martin with liquor provided by the Martin Freres, formerly Fields Stores. The church ushers, young Chris and cousin John, then ushered the guests out to the lush garden setting where the photographing session took place.

"The bride in wide-brimmed flouncy lace hat and just-below the knee full-skirted silk lawn dress, bare shoulders, long lace mittens and small bouquet, was very much the modern bride. She stood next to the handsome groom in dark suit and crisply starched white shirt, brought over from his homeland and expertly prepared by his mother. The couple fingered their matching gold rings as they welcomed the multitude of guests.

"Photos in the garden. Bride with groom. Father and bride. Family group as in the reception line. Bride with bridesmaids, Bibbie's seventeen year old youngest, Lollie and Evie's thirteen years olds, all dressed to match the bride's gown in blue, pink or lavender.

"The cake was cut, speeches made and champagne poured. The sumptuous spread was attacked. The bride and groom opened and displayed their presents. A congratulatory telegram from the California Beauty Pageant was read aloud. What a lovely surprise!

"Time to leave. The bride descended the stairs in her smart going-away outfit and threw her bouquet to the blushing girls below. The bachelors fought for the far-flung garter!

"The chauffeur-driven car was suitably fitted with an old shoe on its rear bumper. Confetti was thrown at the happy couple who dashed to the car which sped up the street in an effort to lose the host of cousins and friends pursuing in their own vehicles.

"The social occasion was a brilliant success!"

"And," added Jill in a loud stage whisper. "the honeymoon was almost a complete disaster!"

CHAPTER 32

"What do you mean, Jill?" asked Horst. "I thought we got through things pretty well. Everything was smooth-sailing from then on, wasn't it?" He trailed off as Jill burst out laughing.

"But, don't you remember when we left the reception to drive to the hotel there was a chain of eight or so cars of cousins and friends following us through London, all tooting madly. Then when Mike, who was driving us, stopped abruptly at a red light and all eight cars rear-ended each other. Remember that? Mike drove off and left everyone behind in a big heap of buckled chrome as they yelled and screamed hilariously as they waved us off!"

It all flooded back to Horst as he took up the story. "We then went up to the hotel in the heart of London, a very posh one, where Mike dropped us off. What a hot day it was, too. As we walked into the lobby and went to register, confetti dropped off us as we swayed, slightly tipsy from all the champagne. The clerk looked at us rather disdainfully. It was a very quiet Sunday afternoon. Well, we registered and they handed over the key to our room, which when we got up there, was so tiny and airless with only one little window looking onto a central well. And you know what a fresh air fiend, I am, don't you, Jill," he added wistfully.

"Yes, don't I just," answered Jill, thinking of the open windows and draughts she had endured all in the name of fresh air. "Then," she reminded him, "you said that you had to go and get something, whatever it was, I don't remember. You'd taken off your jacket and shoes, said, 'Oh, won't be a minute' and rushed off!

"A whole hour went by and you hadn't come back. I began to get worried, knowing you were a bit tipsy and had no shoes or money. I couldn't imagine where you had disappeared to, so I called down to the desk to ask if they had seen you. They hadn't, so I kept on looking down the corridor to see if you'd collapsed somewhere. Then suddenly you appeared at the door, looking very hot and disheveled, and rather shamefaced. As you threw yourself on the bed…" Jill stopped for a moment as Horst's face displayed a revelation of remembrance… "and you said," she continued emphatically, 'Oh my goodness,' or some German phrase. 'I went down to buy some cigarettes and forgot which room we were in. I've been wandering up and down every corridor of the entire hotel, about 500 rooms, I think.'

"Apparently you didn't have the nerve to ask at the front desk, dressed as you were, shoeless and covered in confetti, so went along every corridor hoping to recognize the room," asked Jill, an amazed look on her face. "Did you knock on any doors, or what," she asked, now curious.

"No," replied Horst. "I only peeped into open doors. Of course, I finally did have to go down to the desk and they very suspiciously gave me the number of our room. It was a new clerk on duty, which complicated the issue, too. Phew!" Horst chuckled, his eyes lighting up with another memory. "That reminds me of another incident. Remember the priest gave us some sanctified coins during the wedding ceremony?" Jill had forgotten. "Well," continued Horst, warming to the subject. "When we ordered some cool drinks to be brought up, I accidentally tipped the waiter with those special coins which were supposed to last a life-time." He grimaced.

"Well, I've got something to top that," said Jill mysteriously. "I can laugh now, but at the time it wasn't a laughing matter." Horst urged her on.

"Well, remember how you said to me, 'I feel rather worried about Mama being all alone at the reception, not speaking any English and coming all that long way to a foreign country.' I tried to reassure you that at least she had your sister with her. But you said, 'Even so, I'd like to talk to her on the telephone to see if she's okay.' I tried to stop you for I knew the reaction it would cause. I didn't say any more as you insisted on going ahead."

You dialed the house and my heart was in my mouth. I knew exactly what was going to happen and prayed that someone discreet would answer the phone. As luck would have it, whoever was close to the phone and picked up the receiver, yelled out to the merry-making party, 'Horst wants his mother. He wants to talk to his mother urgently. Where is Horst's mother?' Jill laughed off the incident as she told it, although Horst wasn't inclined to join in. "Of course we can laugh hilariously about it now, can't we?" she continued. "Your mother felt rather embarrassed amongst all the laughter, and I think cut you short. I can tell that my mother wasn't too happy, either." Jill was silent for a moment as she remembered that moment's mortification in the hotel room and the ribald laughter at the family reception.

"Still," she added lightly, "you were the one who was really in trouble that night, weren't you, liebling? Remember how we couldn't sleep in that hot airless cubicle of a room...and you started getting terrible stomach pains and moaned all night long. The worst one of our lives, I think, and supposed to be the best—the honeymoon!"

Horst groaned, glad to get off the other subject. "How could I forget. In the morning too, I remembered that it was Mama's birthday and she was returning to Germany to go on holiday with Papa. I crawled into Selfridge's department store next door to buy her a silver souvenir teaspoon of London. Then we made our weary way through the heat and the pain back to your Mother's by train. I know we really felt like the prodigals returning, especially me, all doubled up in agony." He grimaced at the painful remembrance.

"Mama straight away took care of you," continued Jill. "She knew exactly what to do. 'Get to bed' she said. 'Lie down. No smoking. Proper diet. No drinking. Behave yourself, almost as if she'd been through it all before," said Jill pointedly.

"She also gave me a hot compress on my stomach," added Horst softly.

Jill continued without a pause. "Your mother said, 'I'm leaving. I have a train to catch. Your sister's going to stay on longer. Get fit and well. You're a married man now and have responsibility.'"

"She also said she would have liked to stay on and take care of me," said Horst, even quieter still.

Jill was racing on. "Then I remember watching her go off carrying a large, long mirror wrapped in newspaper. It must have been a present from someone and we'd asked her to take it to Germany for us. We'd hidden all the money we'd received as wedding presents. Remember we'd asked for money rather than gifts as we had no idea where or when we were going to settle down. So we'd hidden all the pound notes in the back of the mirror. We were only allowed to take a very small amount of currency out of England at the time." Jill paused. "I can see her now, carrying this huge mirror under her arm, going all way across Europe by train and boat."

"Yes," interrupted Horst, "and years later she told me what a tortuous thing it was to lug that mirror on and off trains trying not to break it. She wasn't worried about Customs, just that darned mirror breaking her back!" Jill, aghast at Horst's confession—he'd never mentioned it before—raised her voice and her arm in a salute and said "Good, gallant Mama!"

"Shortly after that, remember my parents went off on their pre-arranged holiday," said Jill. "They left Mike and your sister, you and I, in charge of the house and the cat that had just had a litter of kittens. Peter was living in a flat in Earls Court at the time. Your ever-starving sister ate buttered toast non-stop, an expensive feast in Germany at the time, leaving none for the rest of us. As the housekeeper, I was quite furious."

"We four also took off in the car and drove to the coast for an overnighter. Remember how the innkeeper didn't believe that we were married, so we girls took the room while you and Mike went off to get some food."

"And," roared Horst with laughter as he took up the story, "all we could afford was toast and butter! Then we came back after dark and crept up the stairs to the room. The innkeeper kept knocking on the wall all night long to stop our laughter and yelled out asking who was in their with you two girls. Fortunately Mike and I crept out before dawn next morning."

"What a trip that was—and what an ending it had, too," said Jill. "When we got back, the cat had run amok with her kittens through the house. Remember the smell that greeted us—and the clearing up!"

Laughing hilariously, they started to collect the scattered albums and photos from the floor. As they flexed their cramped limbs, Jill turned to Horst. "Remember how on board the Channel-crossing ferry, after we'd make quite a little ceremony of exchanging our rings onto the other hand in the official German way, we thought that everything was behind us and we had nothing but good times to look forward to?"

"It wasn't quite to be, was it," replied Horst. "That's when I really fell ill. The ulcer perforated shortly after our arrival in Ludwigshafen."

Jill remembered that not long after their honeymoon train ride through the Rhein river valley where they stopped in all the historical romantic spots and on arrival how she quickly got a job at the American Air Force base in Heidelberg, that Horst fell ill. How helpless she'd felt on seeing her young husband bent over and staggering, his face creased in pain as he leaned upon his mother. Strong and diminutive beneath his tall, thin frame, Mama helped him down those long flights of stairs to the waiting ambulance. He'd looked like the old man his father was supposed to be—Papa, who had been unable to come over with Mama for the wedding, partly because of his demanding position with the Police Force, but mainly because of his advanced age. How curious Jill had been to meet this man, who at age fifty-five, an age comparable to her fit and frisky parents, was already considered an old man.

"Yes, those were grim days. You know, Papa was very distressed as he watched you leave for the hospital," Jill told Horst. "He stood at the door sighing and shaking his head quite forlornly. Six long weeks you were there, and we were newly-weds."

She thought to herself how she had telephoned to relay the sad news to her mother in London and to hear the reply, "Why don't you come home, dear!" Astonished that her mother could make such a suggestion, she remembers her reply. "Oh, Mother, this is my home now. I wouldn't dream of leaving!"

Standing there, loaded down with their mementoes, Jill touched a fingertip to Horst's arm. "Mama was very kind to me during that time, you know. We used to go for long walks arm in arm. I remember going to the big market place with her and telling her in my poor German how pleased and grateful I was to have her with me."

Poor Mama, thought Jill, who had finally told her son to tell his wife not to prance around their sedate Rhein Valley city in her blue California pedal pusher pants and Indian moccasins. It was quite unseemly that her son's wife would dress so, especially since the neighbours were curious to meet the bride the oldest son had brought back from his short visit to England!

"Still," ventured Horst, wishing to unload, sit down again or go downstairs, "everything worked out, didn't it? Even the trip back to your parents for Christmas. I know that meant a lot to you."

Jill nodded and smiled, realizing that Horst had forgotten the first confrontation with her mother-in-law. It was all over a language problem. But Jill remembered it word for word as if it were yesterday and where she and Mama had been standing in the kitchen, the heart of the home with its mouth-watering aromas that greeted the weary home-bound after the exhausting climb up those eight flights of stairs. She hadn't dreamed it at all!

"But, Horst," she remembers saying, "I'm sure that's what Mama said to me. She said she would help us with the fare money to go over to my parents at Christmas. I'd just told her we wouldn't have enough money from my wages in time to reserve the train and boat. I know my German isn't very good, but Mama repeated it very slowly that she would give us the extra money. And she knew I had understood her when I hugged and thanked her for her generosity and help." This outburst came after Horst had informed her that Mama knew nothing of said conversation and that they were not going to get the money.

Had she misunderstood so completely? Mama would never have changed her mind, or if she had, why hadn't she told her? But then, maybe, feeling a little homesick and wanting so much to do the trip, Jill had only heard what she wished to hear.

"You know, Horst, when I come to think of it, your long hospitalization did have some redeeming value after all, apart from making you well again. It helped bring me a lot closer to your parents in our shared anxiety and my loneliness. My German certainly improved from necessity. You, my life-line to conversation, were in hospital. So, for me it was do or die! No-one could speak English, and Papa only ever quoted 'The Boy Stood on the Burning Deck' and other ancient poems."

Horst broke in. "And didn't he always come to you dictionary in hand for a translation, apart from dreaded Latin proverbs?"

"And, don't forget, too, Horst, that during your absence I was able to borrow a typewriter to type all those complicated German addresses on hundreds of envelopes to earn the extra money for our Christmas trip to London." Horst thought for a moment as he started to go down the stairs. But Jill restrained him.

"Of course, you know what finally brought it all together, don't you, Horst?" She rushed on. "It was when we discovered shortly after our lovely trip to England that Christmas, that number one son was on the way. Remember how proud we were and how we couldn't wait to tell Mama and Papa." She paused, knowing what he was thinking. "Of course, I can understand their reaction now, having gone through three years of raising their first grandchild. Yet, hearing those words and seeing their worried faces, 'Oh no, oh dear. We'll do all we can to help, but don't expect us to raise it for you.' It really upset and horrified me that they thought I'd ask them to do such a thing. I think it was then and there that I decided we should move to England. This was confirmed when I phoned Mother to break the happy news. 'How lovely,' she said. 'I'm going to start a baby jar and save all my sixpences for the baby's arrival!'

Loaded down with their treasures, Jill turned to Horst and said quietly, "Those were the good old times, weren't they?" He nodded.

"We've really had enough for today. We're both so stiff from crouching down for such a long time. My arms and voice are tired, too. We'll look at the rest of the albums some other day."

And down the wooden hill they went.

This memoir is dedicated to all family members and friends no longer with us--our grandparents, parents, aunts and uncles, cousin Barbara, my brother Mike, and most of all my dear husband, Horst, and our beloved Stefan, the first born of our three sons.

Made in the USA
San Bernardino, CA
10 February 2014